AIR FRYER COOKBOOK

Lisa Olson

Warning-Disclaimer

The purpose of this book is to educate and entertain. The author or publisher does not guarantee that anyone following the directions techniques, suggestions, tips, ideas, or strategies will achieve the same results. The author and publisher shall have neither liability or responsibility to anyone with respect to any loss or damage caused, or alleged to be caused, directly or indirectly by the information contained in this book.

CONTENTS

INTRODUCTION

If you believe that there's no such thing as a healthy fried food, think twice! How about an AIR FRYER?! An Air Fryer is a versatile and intelligent kitchen machine with patented technology that utilizes super-heated air to cook food. The machine heats up in a minute; hot air circulates in the specialized chamber so the food is cooked evenly, using a limited amount of oil.

Choosing air frying doesn't mean skimping on flavor. In fact, it means aiming for the healthier versions of our favorite fried foods! For instance, vegetables are one of the healthiest and most nutritious foods. The same cannot be said for deep fried vegetables – they are linked to heart diseases, obesity, diabetes, cancer and other serious health problems.

When it comes to crispy, flavorful and healthy food, it's hard to beat an Air Fryer. You will be able to prepare an entire meal with just one kitchen device. You will be pleasantly surprised what this incredible machine can do for you! Therefore, to put it in a nutshell, if you like your food fried and healthy, an Air Fryer is worth investing in.

BEFORE YOU BUY
AN AIR FRYER

The growing global awareness of healthy eating has encouraged manufacturers to produce more intelligent and more efficient kitchen gadgets for healthy eating. Modern people are constantly looking for new methods of cooking in order to protect their health, prolong life and slow the ageing process naturally. The solution lies in the right dietary regimen as well as in the right cooking method. Thus, Air Fryer is given a place of honor on the kitchen countertop!

When it comes to the benefits and features of an Air Fryer, it would be good to find out more about the anatomy of an Air Fryer.

One of the greatest parts of an Air Fryer, besides the heating element, is the cooking basket. It has a non-stick coating and a mesh bottom; it is perfect for rapid air flow during the cooking process. Located in a sealed environment, the basket allows even distribution of heat through the food.

Furthermore, Air Fryer has a digital screen and touch panel so you can easily set the cooking time and the temperature. Air Fryer features an automatic temperature control so that you don't have to stir your food and slave over a hot stove.

In addition, there is also an exhaust system that regulates the pressure inside the chamber. Moreover, Air Fryer features timer, buzzer and cooking presets (it allows you to choose your desired preset because cooking specifications are previously determined and pre-programmed).

Besides frying, you have the opportunity to bake, steam, roast and grill your food in an Air Fryer. When it comes to baking, you should use a baking dish that is compatible with your model. In most Air Fryer models, you can use oven-safe materials such as glass, metal, and silicone. Grill pan, as its name suggests, allows you to grill and sear the meat and vegetables; it is suitable for multipurpose cooking and it also saves your time, making clean-up a cinch!

There are other versatile Air Fryer accessories on the market such as a double layer rack with skewers, baking inserts, basket dividers, pizza pans, etc.

Air Fryers are easy to use in any home. With its unique design and auto safety feature, in today's rapidly changing world, a hot-air-fryer is a must-have for the household.

How does it work in practice?

Simply place your ingredients into the cooking basket; drizzle some oil, set the timer and the cooking temperature, and voila! Here's the secret of getting more leisure time! Air Fryers actually use electrical power to create their heat. It really is as simple as that! We can only conclude that air frying is an extraordinary way to prepare delicious meals in less time!

If you are looking for better, healthier and more economical options for cooking food on a daily basis, the Air Fryer is the answer!

HOW YOU WILL BENEFIT FROM YOUR AIR FRYER

You simply cannot imagine your life without burgers and chips but you hate all those extra calories in them!

Most people believe that healthy cooking requires a lot of effort, money and special culinary skills, which is why they opt for fast food. But, if you are in possession of the right kitchen tools, cooking becomes a breeze. You can whip up the entire meal in a few minutes and cook it in less than 15 minutes. Try "fix-it and forget-it" air-fried meals and see for yourself.

There are a few obvious benefits of using an Air Fryer.

1. A genius way to save time in the kitchen.

Every day cooking can get burdensome. If you think that cooking at home is time-consuming, here is one of the best time-saving cooking tips: you probably don't have the right kitchen equipment. From now on, you can cook an entire meal in your Air Fryer using its easy press-and-go operation. There is an amazing possibility to cook two different types of food by using an Air Fryer divider. Incredible!

Air Fryer has proven to be the most efficient kitchen companion of those home chefs who don't want to spend all day in the kitchen but want to offer nourishing homemade meals to their families. For instance, it can take about 50 minutes to roast a chicken in a conventional oven. In the Air Fryer, it gets cooked in 30 minutes.

An Air Fryer definitely cuts down cooking time because it heats up very quickly. It takes about 3 to 5 minutes. However, this is optional and you can cook your food immediately, without preheating.

2. Is there such a thing as a healthy fried food?

Speaking realistically, who doesn't love chips, fritters, or croquettes?! Nevertheless, nobody loves excess calories in their stomach and greasy mess in the kitchen and the dining room.

Many studies have proven that vegetable oils release cancer-causing toxic chemicals at high temperatures. We usually use sunflower oil, canola oil, safflower oil, soybean oil, cottonseed oil, corn oil, and other oils to fry with. Cooking with these vegetable oils can be harmful for your health. It is usually linked to serious diseases such as diabetes, heart disease, reproductive problems, cancer, and even hormonal issues and mental decline.

According to the leading experts, we should use olive oil, coconut oil, butter and even tallow and lard. This is the exact way of eating that an Air Fryers promotes – more health-conscious way to cook our favorite foods.

One of the greatest benefits of owning an Air Fryer is the possibility to cook favorite fried food in a much healthier way. These great little appliances cook crispy food without unhealthy additives like vegetable oil. In addition, food is more flavorful because it retains its natural taste, texture and nutrients. Thus, everyone who wants to eat healthier prepared food should consider purchasing an Air Fryer.

3. The ultimate solution to losing weight.

Deep fried food with a massive amount of fat is not a good idea, especially if you want to lose weight or stay fit. For successful weight loss, you should aim to boost flavors and cut calories down. It doesn't mean that you have to avoid terrific fish, saucy steaks, mouthwatering beans, scrumptious cakes, and other treats. You don't need an expensive cookware or special skills. You just need to choose a healthy-cooking technique. An Air Fryer could be a wise kitchen companion in maintaining a healthy weight. Air frying requires less fat compared to other cooking methods, making it one of the best and heathiest cooking methods. Useful nutrients are conserved because of the hot closed environment. At the same time, flavors are more concentrated. Win-win!

Take fried salmon fillets for example. Per 100g, pan fried salmon fillets have 371 calories and 25 grams of fat; oven-baked salmon fillets have 157 calories and 6.96 grams of fat; lastly, air-fried salmon fillets contain 132 calories and 6.2 grams of fat.

Cut calories but not the flavor, and you won't be left with cravings!

4. Cleanup becomes a breeze!

Many people don't fry at home because they are sick and tired of dirty pans and fryers. With an Air Fryer, chicken nuggets, breaded cutlet, pork ribs and dessert are back on the menu!

Air Fryer Cookbook

It's much easier to clean the Air Fryer basket than the pans, deep fryer and the oven. For instance, you should clean the Air Fryer coil four times a year. In addition, the Air Fryer has dishwasher safe parts.

Besides being economical, the Air Fryer is fun! Your kids will run to the kitchen every single time they smell chips or muffins. Bring them into the kitchen and start cooking as a family!

7 TIPS FOR GETTING THE MOST OUT OF YOUR AIR FRYER

Welcome to the Air Fryer meals! Welcome to the gourmet fast food! The Air Fryer is an all-in-one for quick and easy cooking, and once you get to know your device, it opens up a whole new perspective of cooking.

1. Vegetables are one of the easiest foods to cook in your Air Fryer. A wide variety of vegetables can be cooked in the Air Fryer, from delicate beans to root vegetables. For the best results, firstly, soak the vegetables, especially the harder ones, in cold water for 10 to 20 minutes. Next, dry them using a clean kitchen towel.

2. When it comes to the cooking time, it will vary depending on the Air Fryer model, the size of food, its pre-preparation, etc. For shorter cooking times, you should preheat your machine for about 3 minutes; otherwise, if you put the ingredients into the cold cooking basket, the cooking times will be increased with 3 minutes.

3. Keep in mind that you should always try your food for doneness because the recipes are flexible and they are designed for all Air Fryer models. A food thermometer might help to make cooking easier.

4. Yes, you can bake in your Air Fryer but always check with the machine's manual before using new bakeware with your device.

5. Use a good quality oil spray to brush your food and cooking basket; it is also beneficial for easy cleanup.

6. Roasting with air is a new culinary trend you have to try because you can finally prepare your winter favorites and eat them without guilt! Nutritionist Anita Bean said, "When roasting in the Air Fryer, the fat can drop out of the meat, which is a great way of cutting calories."

7. If the recipe calls for ingredients with different cooking time, your Air Fryer is the right tool to cook them perfectly all together. Firstly, put the ingredients that require a longer cooking time; then, you should open your cooker, check the ingredients for doneness and add the food that cooks faster; otherwise, you can overcook your food. If you are not sure about cooking time, feel free to experiment by using the shorter cooking time first. Ultimately, you can set the timer again and cook for another few minutes.

GUIDE TO USING THIS RECIPE COLLECTION

If you want to eat better and healthier, but you are confused by all the information out there, this recipe collection may help you become a great home cook! The cookbook contains 165 recipes that are divided into 10 categories so everyone can gain the benefits. Whether you are a vegan or meat eater, the Air Fryer offers a lot of tasty cooking solutions for you!

If you have no culinary skills and you are afraid of a failure, this recipe collection is ready to be your steady kitchen companion. These appetizing recipes will make your air frying experience more enjoyable and creative! First and foremost, you will use the ingredients that you most likely already have in your kitchen. Then, every recipe contains detailed step-by-step instructions, the number of servings, and cooking time so you can happily indulge into a cooking experience. On the other hand, if you are an experienced home cook, you can ensure that your family eats healthy, wholesome meals. In addition, every recipe contains the nutritional information so that you would have useful facts about the food you cook. Further, this recipe collection is chock-full of great tips such as innovations, substitutions, serving ideas, and so on.

You can experiment with these recipes. Just consult the cooking time chart and try to use ingredients that have similar cooking times if possible. Understanding how an Air Fryer works will help you successfully adapt every single recipe. Don't be afraid to experiment and you will create your own culinary masterpieces in the Air Fryer!

These recipes will make their way to your table with results that satisfy.

Bon appétit!

VEGETABLES & SIDE DISHES

9

5

12

2

15

1. SAUCY SWEET POTATOES WITH ZUCCHINI AND PEPPERS

4 Servings

Ready in about 20 minutes

PER SERVING:
225 Calories; 12.9g Fat;
27.3g Carbs; 2.8g Protein;
8.8g Sugars

It's time to say welcome to the vegetable season! This rich and comfort food is packed with nutrients and amazing natural flavors. Enjoy!

Ingredients

- 2 large-sized sweet potatoes, peeled and quartered
- 1 medium-sized zucchini, sliced
- 1 Serrano pepper, deveined and thinly sliced
- 1 bell pepper, deveined and thinly sliced
- 1-2 carrots, cut into matchsticks
- 1/4 cup olive oil

- 1 ½ tablespoon maple syrup
- 1/2 teaspoon porcini powder
- 1/4 teaspoon mustard powder
- 1/2 teaspoon fennel seeds
- 1 tablespoon garlic powder
- 1/2 teaspoon fine sea salt
- 1/4 teaspoon ground black pepper
- Tomato ketchup, to serve

Directions

1. Place the sweet potatoes, zucchini, peppers, and the carrot into the Air Fryer cooking basket.

2. Drizzle with olive oil and toss to coat; cook in the preheated machine at 350 degrees F for 15 minutes.

3. While the vegetables are cooking, prepare the sauce by thoroughly whisking the other ingredients, without the tomato ketchup. Lightly grease a baking dish that fits into your machine.

4. Transfer cooked vegetables to the prepared baking dish; add the sauce and toss to coat well.

5. Turn the machine to 390 degrees F and cook the vegetables for 5 more minutes. Serve warm with tomato ketchup on the side. Bon appétit!

2. HERBED POTATOES WITH MEDITERRANEAN DIPPING SAUCE

4 Servings

Ready in about
55 minutes

PER SERVING:
295 Calories; 12.3g Fat;
38.4g Carbs; 8.7g Protein;
4.1g Sugars

Mediterranean herbs, such as rosemary and thyme, work well with Russet potatoes.
Further, mascarpone has a very smooth and rich texture that makes your dipping
sauce outstanding! An excellent combo!

Ingredients

- 2 pounds Russet potatoes, peeled and cubed
- 1 ½ tablespoons melted butter
- 1 teaspoon sea salt flakes
- 1 sprig rosemary, leaves only, crushed
- 2 sprigs thyme, leaves only, crushed
- 1/2 teaspoon freshly cracked black peppercorns

For Mediterranean Dipping Sauce:
- 1/2 cup mascarpone cheese
- 1/3 cup yogurt
- 1 tablespoon fresh dill, chopped
- 1 tablespoon olive oil

Directions

1. Firstly, set your Air Fryer to cook at 350 degrees F. Now, add the potato cubes to the bowl with cold water and soak them approximately for 35 minutes.

2. After that, dry the potato cubes using a paper towel.

3. In a mixing dish, thoroughly whisk the melted butter with sea salt flakes, rosemary, thyme, and freshly cracked peppercorns. Rub the potato cubes with this butter/spice mix.

4. Air-fry the potato cubes in the cooking basket for 18 to 20 minutes or until cooked through; make sure to shake the potatoes to cook them evenly.

5. Meanwhile, make the Mediterranean dipping sauce by mixing the remaining ingredients. Serve warm potatoes with Mediterranean sauce for dipping and enjoy!

Air Fryer Cookbook | Vegetables and Side Dishes

8 Servings

Ready in about
30 minutes

PER SERVING:
231 Calories; 3.3g Fat;
41.4g Carbs; 8.7g Protein;
4.5g Sugars

When your friends are visiting, consider preparing these great low-calorie onion rings that are sure to please. Feel free to experiment with herbs and spices.

Ingredients

- 2 medium-sized yellow onions, cut into rings
- 2 cups white flour
- 1/2 teaspoon baking soda
- 1 teaspoon baking powder
- 1 ½ teaspoons sea salt flakes
- 2 medium-sized eggs

- 1 ½ cups plain milk
- 1 ¼ cups seasoned breadcrumbs
- 1/2 teaspoon green peppercorns, freshly cracked
- 1/2 teaspoon dried dill weed
- 1/4 teaspoon paprika

Directions

1. Begin by preheating your Air Fryer to 356 degrees F.

2. Place the onion rings into the bowl with icy cold water; let them stay 15 to 20 minutes; drain the onion rings and dry them using a kitchen towel.

3. In a shallow bowl, mix the sifted flour together with baking soda, baking powder and sea salt flakes. Then, coat each onion ring with the flour mixture;

4. In another shallow bowl, beat the eggs with milk; add the mixture to the remaining flour mixture and whisk well. Dredge the coated onion rings into this batter.

5. In a third bowl, mix the seasoned breadcrumbs, green peppercorns, dill, and paprika. Roll the onion rings over the breadcrumb mix, covering well.

6. Air-fry them in the cooking basket for 8 to 11 minutes or until thoroughly cooked to golden.

4. ROMA TOMATO BITES WITH HALLOUMI CHEESE

4 Servings

Ready in about
20 minutes

PER SERVING:
428 Calories; 38.4g Fat;
4.5g Carbs; 18.8g Protein;
2.3g Sugars

This is a delicious spicy side dish on its own, as well as a great addition to the main dishes such as crispy fish fingers or Mediterranean herbed chicken. Enjoy!

Ingredients

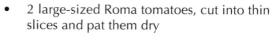

For the Sauce:

- 1/2 cup Parmigiano-Reggiano cheese, grated
- 4 tablespoons pecans, chopped
- 1 teaspoon garlic puree
- 1/2 teaspoon fine sea salt
- 1/3 cup extra-virgin olive oil

For the Tomato Bites:

- 2 large-sized Roma tomatoes, cut into thin slices and pat them dry
- 8 ounces Halloumi cheese, cut into thin slices
- 1/3 cup onions, sliced
- 1 teaspoon dried basil
- 1/4 teaspoon red pepper flakes, crushed
- 1/8 teaspoon sea salt

Directions

1. Start by preheating your Air Fryer to 385 degrees F.

2. Make the sauce by mixing all ingredients, except the extra-virgin olive oil, in your food processor.

3. While the machine is running, slowly and gradually pour in the olive oil; puree until everything is well - blended.

4. Now, spread 1 teaspoon of the sauce over the top of each tomato slice. Place a slice of Halloumi cheese on each tomato slice. Top with onion slices. Sprinkle with basil, red pepper, and sea salt.

5. Transfer the assembled bites to the Air Fryer cooking basket. Drizzle with a nonstick cooking spray and cook for approximately 13 minutes.

6. Arrange these bites on a nice serving platter, garnish with the remaining sauce and serve at room temperature. Bon appétit!

5. EASY SAUTÉED GREEN BEANS

4 Servings

Ready in about
12 minutes

PER SERVING:
53 Calories; 3.0g Fat;
6.1g Carbs; 1.6g Protein;
1.2g Sugars

Regardless of whether you are using fresh or frozen green beans, they contain many valuable nutrients. If you prefer hotter foods, add chili pepper or hot paprika to this recipe.

Ingredients

- 3/4 pound green beans, cleaned
- 1 tablespoon balsamic vinegar
- 1/4 teaspoon kosher salt

- 1/2 teaspoon mixed peppercorns, freshly cracked
- 1 tablespoon butter
- Sesame seeds, to serve

Directions

1. Set your Air Fryer to cook at 390 degrees F.

2. Mix the green beans with all of the above ingredients, apart from the sesame seeds. Set the timer for 10 minutes.

3. Meanwhile, toast the sesame seeds in a small-sized nonstick skillet; make sure to stir continuously.

4. Serve sautéed green beans on a nice serving platter sprinkled with toasted sesame seeds. Bon appétit!

4 Servings

Ready in about
15 minutes

PER SERVING:
290 Calories; 14.4g Fat;
32.5g Carbs; 10.7g
Protein; 1.4g Sugars

Serve these stuffed potatoes that are bursting with flavor as a light dinner or a side dish. Simply add an aromatic fresh salad and enjoy!

Ingredients

- 4 baking potatoes
- 2 tablespoons olive oil
- 1/2 cup Ricotta cheese, room temperature
- 2 tablespoons scallions, chopped
- 1 heaping tablespoon fresh parsley, roughly chopped

- 1 heaping tablespoon coriander, minced
- 2 ounces Cheddar cheese, preferably freshly grated
- 1 teaspoon celery seeds
- 1/2 teaspoon salt
- 1/2 teaspoon garlic pepper

Directions

1. Firstly, prick your potatoes with a small paring knife. Cook them in the Air Fryer cooking basket for approximately 13 minutes at 350 degrees F. Check for doneness and cook for 2-3 minutes longer if needed.

2. Meanwhile, make the stuffing by mixing the other items.

3. When your potatoes are thoroughly cooked, open them up. Divide the stuffing among all potatoes and serve on individual plates.

7. EASY CHEESY CAULIFLOWER AND BROCCOLI

6 Servings

Ready in about
20 minutes

PER SERVING:
133 Calories; 9.0g Fat;
9.5g Carbs; 5.9g Protein;
3.2g Sugars

As hearty whole foods, cauliflower and broccoli have many health benefits. If you are looking for a quick and light vegetarian meal, try this recipe! You will make it again and again!

Ingredients

- 1 pound cauliflower florets
- 1 pound broccoli florets
- 2 ½ tablespoons sesame oil
- 1/2 teaspoon smoked cayenne pepper

- 3/4 teaspoon sea salt flakes
- 1 tablespoon lemon zest, grated
- 1/2 cup Colby cheese, shredded

Directions

1. Prepare the cauliflower and broccoli using your favorite steaming method. Then, drain them well; add the sesame oil, cayenne pepper, and salt flakes.

2. Air-fry at 390 degrees F for approximately 16 minutes; make sure to check the vegetables halfway through the cooking time.

3. Afterwards, stir in the lemon zest and Colby cheese; toss to coat well and serve immediately!

2 Servings

Ready in about
15 minutes

PER SERVING:
317 Calories; 19.8g
Fat; 16.5g Carbs; 20.1g
Protein; 10.2g Sugars

This is one of the best advantages of an Air Fryer. You can simply place your favorite ingredients into the pan and wait for the machine to do the rest.

Ingredients

- 3 tablespoons plain milk
- 4 eggs, whisked
- 1 teaspoon melted butter
- Kosher salt and freshly ground black pepper, to taste
- 1 red bell pepper, deveined and chopped

- 1 green bell pepper, deveined and chopped
- 1 white onion, finely chopped
- 1/2 cup baby spinach leaves, roughly chopped
- 1/2 cup Halloumi cheese, shaved

Directions

1. Start with spreading the canola cooking spray onto the Air Fryer baking pan.

2. Add all of the above ingredients to the baking pan; give them a good stir.

3. Then, set your machine to cook at 350 degrees F; cook your omelet for 13 minutes. Serve warm and enjoy!

9. MUSHROOMS AND PEPPERS IN PUFF PASTRY

4 Servings

Ready in about
25 minutes

PER SERVING:
533 Calories; 38.7g Fat;
39.1g Carbs; 8.4g Protein;
2.5g Sugars

Elegant pastries filled with vegetables and cream make a great family dinner. As a matter of fact, puff pastry rolls are only limited by your imagination!

Ingredients

- 1 ½ tablespoons sesame oil
- 1 cup sliced white mushrooms
- 2 cloves garlic, minced
- 1 bell pepper, seeded and chopped
- 1/4 teaspoon sea salt
- 1/4 teaspoon dried rosemary

- 1/2 teaspoon ground black pepper, or more to taste
- 11 ounces puff pastry sheets
- 1/2 cup crème fraiche
- 1 egg, well whisked
- 1/2 cup Parmesan cheese, preferably freshly grated

Directions

1. Start by preheating your Air Fryer to 400 degrees F.

2. Then, heat the sesame oil in a skillet that is placed over a moderate heat; cook the mushrooms, garlic, and pepper until tender and fragrant. Season with salt, rosemary, and pepper.

3. Meanwhile, roll out the puff pastry; cut into 4-inch squares. Evenly spread the crème fraiche on them.

4. Then, divide the vegetables among the puff pastry squares. Fold each square diagonally over the filling in order to form a triangle shape. Pinch the edges and coat each triangle with whisked egg. Coat them with grated Parmesan.

5. Cook for 22 to 25 minutes. Bon appétit!

4 Servings

Ready in about
10 minutes

PER SERVING:
124 Calories; 2.0g Fat;
21.9g Carbs; 4.8g Protein;
3.0g Sugars

Everybody loves croquettes! This is the healthy and tasty version of this favorite comfort food. You can "perk up" these croquets with chive mayo but horseradish mayo works well too.

Ingredients

- 2 medium-sized carrots, trimmed and grated
- 2 medium-sized celery stalks, trimmed and grated
- 1/2 cup of leek, finely chopped
- 1 tablespoon garlic paste
- 1/4 teaspoon freshly cracked black pepper
- 1 teaspoon fine sea salt

- 1 tablespoon fresh dill, finely chopped
- 1 egg, lightly whisked
- 1/4 cup all-purpose flour
- 1/4 teaspoon baking powder
- 1/2 cup breadcrumbs (seasoned or regular)
- Chive mayo, to serve

Directions

1. Place the carrots and celery on a paper towel and squeeze them to remove excess liquid.

2. Combine the vegetables with the other ingredients, except the breadcrumbs and chive mayo. Shape the balls using 1 tablespoon of the vegetable mixture.

3. Then, gently flatten each ball with your palm or a wide spatula. Coat them with breadcrumbs, covering all sides. Spritz the croquettes with a non - stick cooking oil.

4. Air-fry the vegetable croquettes in a single layer for 6 minutes at 360 degrees F. Serve warm with chive mayo. Bon appétit!

11. SCRAMBLED EGGS WITH SPINACH AND TOMATO

2 Servings

Ready in about
15 minutes

PER SERVING:
274 Calories; 23.2g Fat;
5.7g Carbs; 13.7g Protein;
2.6g Sugars

Scrambled eggs aren't just for breakfast. With the addition of healthy veggies, they can be served at any time in order to boost your energy and overall health!

Ingredients

- 2 tablespoons olive oil, melted
- 4 eggs, whisked
- 5 ounces fresh spinach, chopped
- 1 medium-sized tomato, chopped

- 1 teaspoon fresh lemon juice
- 1/2 teaspoon coarse salt
- 1/2 teaspoon ground black pepper
- 1/2 cup of fresh basil, roughly chopped

Directions

1. Add the olive oil to an Air Fryer baking pan. Make sure to tilt the pan to spread the oil evenly.

2. Simply combine the remaining ingredients, except for the basil leaves; whisk well until everything is well incorporated.

3. Cook in the preheated Air Fryer for 8 to 12 minutes at 280 degrees F. Garnish with fresh basil leaves. Serve warm with a dollop of sour cream if desired.

8 Servings

Ready in about
15 minutes

PER SERVING:
291 Calories; 18.0g Fat;
23.7g Carbs; 9.3g Protein;
1.7g Sugars

These old-fashioned potato patties are cheap and easy to make. They are really good to serve with tabasco mayo or any other homemade flavored mayo.

Ingredients

- 2 pounds white potatoes, peeled and grated
- 1/2 cup scallions, finely chopped
- 1/2 teaspoon freshly ground black pepper, or more to taste
- 1 tablespoon fine sea salt

- 1/2 teaspoon hot paprika
- 2 cups Colby cheese, shredded
- 1/4 cup canola oil
- 1 cup crushed crackers

Directions

1. Firstly, boil the potatoes until fork tender. Drain, peel and mash your potatoes.

2. Thoroughly mix the mashed potatoes with scallions, pepper, salt, paprika, and cheese. Then, shape the balls using your hands. Now, flatten the balls to make the patties.

3. In a shallow bowl, mix canola oil with crushed crackers. Roll the patties over the crumb mixture.

4. Next, cook your patties at 360 degrees F approximately 10 minutes, working in batches. Serve with tabasco mayo if desired. Bon appétit!

13. ZESTY BROCCOLI BITES WITH HOT SAUCE

6 Servings

Ready in about
20 minutes

PER SERVING:
80 Calories; 3.8g Fat;
10.8g Carbs; 2.5g Protein;
6.6g Sugars

This recipe calls for a homemade hot sauce that is incredibly easy to make. This sauce features balsamic vinegar for a more vibrant flavor; it goes well with hearty broccoli florets.

Ingredients

For the Broccoli Bites:

- 1 medium-sized head broccoli, broken into florets
- 1/2 teaspoon lemon zest, freshly grated
- 1/3 teaspoon fine sea salt
- 1/2 teaspoon hot paprika
- 1 teaspoon shallot powder
- 1 teaspoon porcini powder
- 1/2 teaspoon granulated garlic
- 1/3 teaspoon celery seeds
- 1 ½ tablespoons olive oil

For the Hot Sauce:

- 1/2 cup tomato sauce
- 3 tablespoons brown sugar
- 1 tablespoon balsamic vinegar
- 1/2 teaspoon ground allspice

Directions

1. Toss all the ingredients for the broccoli bites in a mixing bowl, covering the broccoli florets on all sides.

2. Cook them in the preheated Air Fryer at 360 degrees for 13 to 15 minutes. In the meantime, mix all ingredients for the hot sauce.

3. Pause your Air Fryer, mix the broccoli with the prepared sauce and cook for further 3 minutes. Bon appétit!

14. SWEET CORN AND KERNEL FRITTERS

4 Servings

Ready in about
20 minutes

PER SERVING:
275 Calories; 8.4g Fat;
40.5g Carbs; 15.7g
Protein; 7.3g Sugars

To save time, you can cook some extra fritter cakes for lunch and pack the rest for dinner. It is easy to double this recipe and work in batches when you possess a magical Air Fryer!

Ingredients

- 1 medium-sized carrot, grated
- 1 yellow onion, finely chopped
- 4 ounces canned sweet corn kernels, drained
- 1 teaspoon sea salt flakes
- 1 heaping tablespoon fresh cilantro, chopped

- 1 medium-sized egg, whisked
- 2 tablespoons plain milk
- 1 cup of Parmesan cheese, grated
- 1/4 cup of self-rising flour
- 1/3 teaspoon baking powder
- 1/3 teaspoon brown sugar

Directions

1. Press down the grated carrot in the colander to remove excess liquid. Then, spread the grated carrot between several sheets of kitchen towels and pat it dry.

2. Then, mix the carrots with the remaining ingredients in the order listed above.

3. Roll 1 tablespoon of the mixture into a ball; gently flatten it using the back of a spoon or your hand. Now, repeat with the remaining ingredients.

4. Spitz the balls with a nonstick cooking oil. Cook in a single layer at 350 degrees for 8 to 11 minutes or until they're firm to touch in the center. Serve warm and enjoy!

15. GORGONZOLA STUFFED MUSHROOMS WITH HORSERADISH MAYO

5 Servings

Ready in about
15 minutes

PER SERVING:
210 Calories; 15.2g Fat;
13.6g Carbs; 7.6g Protein;
2.7g Sugars

In this healthy mushroom recipe, Gorgonzola and garlic are added to be prepared an uncommonly rich and flavorful vegetarian dinner. A delicious horseradish mayo emphasizes the flavors.

Ingredients

- 1/2 cup of breadcrumbs
- 2 cloves garlic, pressed
- 2 tablespoons fresh coriander, chopped
- 1/3 teaspoon kosher salt
- 1/2 teaspoon crushed red pepper flakes
- 1 ½ tablespoons olive oil

- 20 medium-sized mushrooms, cut off the stems
- 1/2 cup Gorgonzola cheese, grated
- 1/4 cup low-fat mayonnaise
- 1 teaspoon prepared horseradish, well-drained
- 1 tablespoon fresh parsley, finely chopped

Directions

1. Mix the breadcrumbs together with the garlic, coriander, salt, red pepper, and the olive oil; mix to combine well.

2. Stuff the mushroom caps with the breadcrumb filling. Top with grated Gorgonzola.

3. Place the mushrooms in the Air Fryer grill pan and slide them into the machine. Grill them at 380 degrees F for 8 to 12 minutes or until the stuffing is warmed through.

4. Meanwhile, prepare the horseradish mayo by mixing the mayonnaise, horseradish and parsley. Serve with the warm fried mushrooms. Enjoy!

CHICKEN

28

19

26

17

30

16. CHICKEN WINGS IN PIRI PIRI SAUCE

6 Servings

Ready in about
1 hour 30 minutes

PER SERVING:
381 Calories; 17.6g Fat;
9.3g Carbs; 45.2g Protein;
5.5g Sugars

Recipes with chicken wings are endless. This recipe calls for piri piri that is also called African bird's eye chili. If you want to make this sauce less spicy and hot, just deseed and devein the peppers and simply reduce the number of those that are chili.

Ingredients

- 12 chicken wings
- 1 ½ ounces butter, melted
- 1 teaspoon onion powder
- 1/2 teaspoon cumin powder
- 1 teaspoon garlic paste

For the Sauce:

- 2 ounces piri piri peppers, stemmed and chopped
- 1 tablespoon pimiento, deveined and minced
- 1 garlic clove, chopped
- 2 tablespoons fresh lemon juice
- 1/3 teaspoon sea salt
- 1/2 teaspoon tarragon
- 3/4 teaspoon brown sugar

Directions

1. Steam the chicken wings using a steamer basket that is placed over a saucepan with boiling water; reduce the heat.

2. Now, steam the wings for 10 minutes over a moderate heat. Toss the wings with butter, onion powder, cumin powder, and garlic paste.

3. Let the chicken wings cool to room temperature. Then, refrigerate them for 45 to 50 minutes.

4. Roast in the preheated Air Fryer at 330 degrees F for 25 to 30 minutes; make sure to flip them halfway through.

5. While the chicken wings are cooking, prepare the sauce by mixing all of the sauce ingredients in a food processor. Toss the wings with prepared Piri Piri Sauce and serve.

17. SPRING CHICKEN AND RICOTTA WRAPS

12 Servings

Ready in about
20 minutes

PER SERVING:
468 Calories; 4.6g Fat;
80.4g Carbs; 23.4g
Protein; 1.2g Sugars

Say YES to your favorite fried food! These guilt-free wraps have a little amount of fat but they are still crispy and tasty like those that have been fried in oil.

Ingredients

- 2 large-sized chicken breasts, cooked and shredded
- 1/3 teaspoon sea salt
- 1/4 teaspoon ground black pepper, or more to taste
- 2 spring onions, chopped

- 1/4 cup soy sauce
- 1 tablespoon molasses
- 1 tablespoon rice vinegar
- 10 ounces Ricotta cheese
- 1 teaspoon grated fresh ginger
- 50 wonton wrappers

Directions

1. Combine all of the above ingredients, except the wonton wrappers, in a mixing dish.

2. Lay out the wrappers on a clean surface. Brush them with a nonstick cooking spray. Spread the wonton wrappers with the prepared filling.

3. Fold the outside corners to the center over the filling and roll up every wonton wrapper tightly; you can moisten the edges with a little water.

4. Set the Air Fryer to cook at 375 degrees F. Air-fry the rolls for 5 minutes, working in batches. Serve with a dipping sauce of your choice. Bon appétit!

18. PERFECT CHICKEN SAUSAGE WITH MUSTARD-HONEY SAUCE

4 Servings

Ready in about
20 minutes

PER SERVING:
266 Calories; 8.7g Fat;
12.6g Carbs; 33.4g
Protein; 9.6g Sugars

Air-frying is one of the best and easiest ways to cook the perfect sausages. Meanwhile, just whip up the mustard-honey sauce in less than 5 minutes and enjoy!

Ingredients

- 4 chicken sausages
- 2 tablespoons honey
- 1/4 cup mayonnaise

- 2 tablespoons Dijon mustard
- 1 tablespoon balsamic vinegar
- 1/2 teaspoon dried rosemary

Directions

1. Arrange the sausages on the grill pan and transfer it to the preheated Air Fryer.

2. Grill the sausages at 350 degrees F for approximately 13 minutes. Turn them halfway through cooking.

3. Meanwhile, prepare the sauce by mixing the remaining ingredients with a wire whisk. Serve the warm sausages with chilled mustard-honey sauce. Enjoy!

19. GOURMET CHICKEN OMELET

2 Servings

Ready in about
15 minutes

PER SERVING:
246 Calories; 13.0g Fat;
3.5g Carbs; 28.1g Protein;
1.3g Sugars

This recipe calls for hot sauce but you can omit this ingredient. You can add some vegetables as well – finely chopped peppers and grated zucchini are the sensible choice because the cooking time is the same as for the scallions.

Ingredients

- 4 eggs, whisked
- 4 ounces ground chicken
- 1/2 cup scallions, finely chopped
- 2 cloves garlic, finely minced
- 1/2 teaspoon salt

- 1/2 teaspoon ground black pepper
- 1/2 teaspoon paprika
- 1 teaspoon dried thyme
- A dash of hot sauce

Directions

1. Thoroughly combine all the ingredients in a mixing dish. Now, scrape the egg mixture into two oven safe ramekins that are previously greased with a thin layer of the vegetable oil.

2. Set your machine to cook at 350 degrees F; air-fry for 13 minutes or until thoroughly cooked. Serve immediately.

20. SAUCY TARRAGON CHICKEN

4 Servings

Ready in about
20 minutes

PER SERVING:
221 Calories; 6.0g Fat;
4.0g Carbs; 35.9g Protein;
2.2g Sugars

You can prepare this saucy chicken for a family lunch or for an elegant supper. This is a protein-packed meal so you can serve it as a muscle-building dinner.

Ingredients

- 2 cups of roasted vegetable broth
- 2 chicken breasts, cut into halves
- 3/4 teaspoon fine sea salt
- 1/4 teaspoon mixed peppercorns, freshly cracked
- 1 teaspoon cumin powder
- 1 ½ teaspoons sesame oil

- 1 ½ tablespoons Worcester sauce
- 1/2 cup of spring onions, chopped
- 1 Serrano pepper, deveined and chopped
- 1 bell pepper, deveined and chopped
- 1 tablespoon tamari sauce
- 1/2 chopped fresh tarragon

Directions

1. Place the vegetable broth and chicken breasts in a deep saucepan; cook for 10 minutes; reduce the temperature and let it simmer for additional 10 minutes.

2. After that, allow the chicken to cool slightly; shred the chicken using a stand mixer or two forks.

3. Toss the shredded chicken with the salt, cracked peppercorns, cumin, sesame oil and the Worcester sauce; air-fry them at 380 degrees F for 18 minutes; check for doneness.

4. Meanwhile, in a non-stick skillet, cook the remaining ingredients over a moderate flame. Cook until the onions and peppers are tender and fragrant.

5. Remove the skillet from the heat, add the shredded chicken and toss to combine.

6. Serve right away!

4 Servings

Ready in about
20 minutes

PER SERVING:
561 Calories; 38.3g Fat;
2.1g Carbs; 49.3g Protein;
0.6g Sugars

It tastes like a pizza without the guilt of having carbs! If this sounds appealing to you, try this irresistible combination of tender chicken fillets, cheese and pepperoni!

Ingredients

- 4 small-sized chicken breasts, boneless and skinless
- 1/4 cup pizza sauce
- 1/2 cup Colby cheese, shredded

- 16 slices pepperoni
- Salt and pepper, to savor
- 1 ½ tablespoons olive oil
- 1 ½ tablespoons dried oregano

Directions

1. Carefully flatten out the chicken breast using a rolling pin.

2. Divide the ingredients among four chicken fillets. Roll the chicken fillets with the stuffing and seal them using a small skewer or two toothpicks.

3. Roast in the preheated Air Fryer grill pan for 13 to 15 minutes at 370 degrees F. Bon appétit!

22. MUSTARD AND TURMERIC CHICKEN THIGHS

6 Servings

Ready in about
20 minutes

PER SERVING:
402 Calories; 16.9g
Fat; 13.4g Carbs; 46.1g
Protein; 1.0g Sugars

This chicken recipe is perfect for any occasion. To serve, drizzle warm fried thighs with remaining marinade for more piquant flavor. Yummy!

Ingredients

- 1 large-sized egg, well whisked
- 2 tablespoons whole-grain Dijon mustard
- 1/4 cup of mayonnaise
- 1/4 cup of chili sauce
- 1/2 teaspoon brown sugar
- 1 teaspoon fine sea salt

- 1/2 teaspoon ground black pepper, or more to taste
- 1/2 teaspoon turmeric powder
- 10 chicken thighs
- 2 cups crushed saltines

Directions

1. Firstly, in a large-sized mixing bowl, thoroughly combine the egg, mustard, mayonnaise, chili sauce, brown sugar, salt, pepper, and turmeric.

2. Add the chicken thighs to the mixing bowl; cover with foil and let them marinate for at least 5 hours or overnight in your fridge.

3. After that, set your Air Fryer to cook at 360 degrees F. Remove the chicken from the marinade.

4. Put the crushed saltines into a shallow dish. Roll the marinated chicken over the crumbs.

5. Set the timer for 15 minutes and cook until the thighs are cooked through. Serve with remaining marinade. Bon appétit!

23. TENDER CHICKEN IN WINE SAUCE

4 Servings

Ready in about
30 minutes

PER SERVING:
367 Calories; 4.0g Fat;
40.1g Carbs; 39.0g
Protein; 19.1g Sugars

Inspired by white cooking wine, you can come up with this recipe that is simply scrumptious! This is a great idea for your next dinner party.

Ingredients

- 2 chicken breasts, cut into bite-sized chunks
- 1/3 cup cornstarch
- 1/3 cup flour
- 1 cup scallions, chopped
- 1 parsnip, chopped
- 1 carrot, thinly sliced

For the Sauce:

- 1/4 cup of honey
- 1/4 cup of dry white wine
- 1/4 cup of soy sauce
- 1/3 cup of chicken broth

Directions

1. Start by preheating your Air Fryer to 365 degrees F. Toss the chicken chunks with the corn starch and flour, covering well.

2. Air-fry the chicken for 20 minutes in the preheated cooker. Pause the Air Fryer and place the vegetables in; cook for a further 5 to 7 minutes.

3. Meanwhile, in a sauté pan, whisk the sauce and the ingredients over a moderate flame; then, turn the heat to medium-low and simmer for 2 to 3 minutes. Serve the chicken with the warm sauce and enjoy!

3 Servings

Ready in about
1 hour 15 minutes

PER SERVING:
359 Calories; 8.6g Fat;
29.7g Carbs; 40.5g
Protein; 24.6g Sugars

Make sure to get a high-quality garam masala for this recipe. This Ayurvedic spice mix does wonders for your health (e.g. it controls your cholesterol levels, protects your teeth, fights against free radicals, etc.)

Ingredients

- 1 tablespoon water
- 1 tablespoon cornstarch
- 1/4 cup soy sauce
- 1/4 cup honey
- 1/4 cup tomato puree
- 1 teaspoon garlic paste

- 1/2 teaspoon fresh ginger, grated
- 3 chicken legs
- 1 tablespoon peanut oil
- 1 teaspoon fresh lemon juice
- 1 teaspoon garam masala
- Sea salt and ground black pepper, to savor

Directions

1. To make the marinade, preheat a sauté pan over a low flame; then, simmer the first seven ingredients until the sauce is reduced to half.

2. Transfer the marinade into a baking dish; add the chicken legs, followed by the remaining ingredients; let them marinate for at least 30 minutes. Now, set your Air Fryer to cook at 390 degrees F.

3. Cook in the preheated Air Fryer for 25 minutes. Then, flip the chicken legs halfway through cooking and cook for another 20 minutes, Taste, fix the seasonings and serve immediately over naan!

25. BUTTERMILK FRIED CHICKEN TENDERS

4 Servings

Ready in about
1 hour 15 minutes

PER SERVING:
436 Calories; 12.7g Fat;
40.5g Carbs;
39.2g Protein; 2.5g Sugars

This is a child-friendly recipe but adults will enjoy it as well. These heavenly delicious chicken tenders go well with roasted sweet potato wedges. Lovely!

Ingredients

- 3/4 cup of buttermilk
- 1 pound chicken tenders
- 1 ½ cups all-purpose flour
- Salt, to your liking
- 1/2 teaspoon pink peppercorns, freshly cracked

- 1 teaspoon shallot powder
- 1/2 teaspoon cumin powder
- 1 ½ teaspoon smoked cayenne pepper
- 1 tablespoon sesame oil

Directions

1. Place the buttermilk and chicken tenders in the mixing dish; gently stir to coat and let it soak for 1 hour.

2. Then, mix the flour with all seasonings. Coat the soaked chicken tenders with the flour mixture; now, dip them into the buttermilk. Finally, dredge them in the flour.

3. Brush the prepared chicken tenders with sesame oil and lower them onto the bottom of a cooking basket.

4. Air-fry for 15 minutes at 365 degrees F; make sure to shake them once or twice. Bon appétit!

26. PENNE WITH CHICKEN SAUSAGE MEATBALLS

4 Servings

Ready in about
20 minutes

PER SERVING:
384 Calories; 5.3g Fat;
60.2g Carbs; 22.5g
Protein; 0.6g Sugars

If you probably already know, ground chicken may be healthier than ground pork or beef. However, this recipe doesn't call for any extra fat and it is a proof that you don't need it for amazing flavor!

Ingredients

- 1 cup chicken meat, ground
- 1 sweet red pepper, minced
- 1/4 cup green onions, chopped
- 1 green garlic, minced
- 4 tablespoons seasoned breadcrumbs

- 1/2 teaspoon cumin powder
- 1 tablespoon fresh coriander, minced
- 1/2 teaspoon sea salt
- 1/4 teaspoon mixed peppercorns, ground
- 1 package penne pasta, cooked

Directions

1. Place the chicken, red pepper, green onions, and garlic into a mixing bowl; mix to combine well.

2. Now, add seasoned breadcrumbs, followed by all seasonings; mix again until everything is well incorporated.

3. Next, shape into small balls (e.g. the size of a golf ball); cook them in the preheated Air Fryer at 350 degrees F for 15 minutes; shaking once or twice to ensure evenness of cooking. Serve over cooked penne pasta.

4 Servings

Ready in about
40 minutes

PER SERVING:
306 Calories; 12.8g Fat;
14.5g Carbs;
32.2g Protein; 1.3g Sugars

If you like crispier skin, cook these wings for 30 minutes. You can also marinate them for a couple of hours for better flavor.

Ingredients

- 4 large-sized chicken wings
- 1 teaspoon Cajun seasoning
- 1 teaspoon maple syrup
- 3/4 teaspoon sea salt flakes
- 1/4 teaspoon red pepper flakes, crushed
- 1 teaspoon onion powder
- 1 teaspoon porcini powder
- 1/2 teaspoon celery seeds
- 1 small-seized head of cabbage, shredded
- 1 cup mashed potatoes

- 1 small-sized brown onion, coarsely grated
- 1 teaspoon garlic puree
- 1 medium-sized whole egg, well whisked
- 1/2 teaspoon table salt
- 1/2 teaspoon ground black pepper
- 1 ½ tablespoons all-purpose flour
- 3/4 teaspoon baking powder
- 1 heaping tablespoon cilantro
- 1 tablespoon sesame oil

Directions

1. Start by preheating your Air Fryer to 390 degrees F. Dry the chicken wings. Now, prepare the rub by mixing Cajun seasoning, maple syrup, sea salt flakes, red pepper, onion powder, porcini powder, and celery seeds.

2. Cook for 25 to 30 minutes or until the wings are no longer pink in the middle.

3. Then, mix the shredded cabbage, potato, onion, garlic puree, egg, table salt, black pepper, flour, baking powder and cilantro in a mixing bowl.

4. Divide the cabbage mixture into 4 portions and create four cabbage/potato cakes. Sprinkle each cake with the sesame oil.

5. Bake cabbage/potato cakes for 10 minutes, flipping them once and working in batches. Finally, serve with the chicken wings and enjoy!

28. MAJESTIC MAPLE-GLAZED CHICKEN

4 Servings

Ready in about
20 minutes +
marinating time

PER SERVING:
189 Calories; 3.1g Fat;
9.1g Carbs; 29.5g Protein;
7.6g Sugars

Using marinated chicken is one of the easiest ways to transform a good-enough chicken recipe into an outstanding royal meal. It would be great if you could marinate the chicken overnight.

Ingredients

- 2 ½ tablespoons maple syrup
- 1 tablespoon tamari soy sauce
- 1 tablespoon oyster sauce
- 1 teaspoon fresh lemon juice

- 1 teaspoon minced fresh ginger
- 1 teaspoon garlic puree
- Seasoned salt and freshly ground pepper, to your liking
- 2 chicken breasts, boneless and skinless

Directions

1. To prepare the marinade, in a mixing dish, combine maple syrup, tamari sauce, oyster sauce, lemon juice, fresh ginger and garlic puree.

2. Now, season the chicken breasts with salt and pepper. Put the chicken breast into the bowl with the marinade and make sure to coat them well; cover with foil and place in the refrigerator for 3 hours or overnight.

3. Discard the marinade. Air-fry marinated chicken breast for 15 minutes at 365 degrees F; turn them once or twice.

4. Meanwhile, add the remaining marinade to a pan that is preheated over a moderate flame; let it simmer until reduced by half; it will take 3 to 5 minutes. Serve the chicken with the sauce. Bon appétit!

29. SAUCY PROVENÇAL CHICKEN WITH BACON

4 Servings

Ready in about
25 minutes

PER SERVING:
296 Calories; 13.7g Fat;
6.9g Carbs; 34.7g Protein;
2.9g Sugars

This chicken drumstick recipe could not be simpler - just place the ingredients into your magical Air Fryer and you will have a great protein meal! In terms of the spice mix called "Herbs de Provence", it typically contains marjoram, rosemary, thyme, savory, oregano and other herbs that grow mainly in southern France.

Ingredients

- 4 medium-sized skin-on chicken drumsticks
- 1 ½ teaspoons herbs de Provence
- Salt and pepper, to your liking
- 1 tablespoon rice vinegar
- 2 tablespoons olive oil

- 2 garlic cloves, crushed
- 12 ounces crushed canned tomatoes
- 1 small-size leek, thinly sliced
- 2 slices smoked bacon, chopped

Directions

1. Sprinkle the chicken drumsticks with herbs de Provence, salt and pepper; then, drizzle them with rice vinegar and olive oil. Cook in the baking pan at 360 degrees F for 8 to 10 minutes.

2. Pause the Air Fryer; stir in the remaining ingredients and continue to cook for 15 minutes longer; make sure to check them periodically. Serve over rice garnished with lemon wedges. Bon appétit!

30. MELT-IN-YOUR-MOUTH MARJORAM CHICKEN

2 Servings

Ready in about
1 hour

PER SERVING:
328 Calories; 16.1g Fat;
0.0g Carbs; 43.6g Protein;
0.0 g Sugars

Nice and easy low-carb meal for two. Therefore, if you love chicken, this recipe will win your heart right now! Serve with a crisp Sauvignon Blanc.

Ingredients

- 2 small-sized chicken breasts, skinless and boneless
- 2 tablespoons butter
- 1 teaspoon sea salt
- 1/2 teaspoon red pepper flakes, crushed
- 2 teaspoons marjoram
- 1/4 teaspoon lemon pepper

Directions

1. Add all of the above ingredients to a mixing dish; let it marinate for 30 minutes to 1 hour.

2. Then, set your Air Fryer to cook at 390 degrees. Cook for 20 minutes, turning halfway through cooking time.

3. Check for doneness using an instant-read thermometer. Serve over jasmine rice. Bon appétit!

TURKEY

38

31

35

43

41

6 Servings

Ready in about
15 minutes

PER SERVING:
241 Calories; 17.5g Fat;
1.1g Carbs; 23.0g Protein;
0.0 g Sugars

These crowd-pleasing and child-friendly meatballs are perfect for any occasion.
They are delicious eye catching!

Ingredients

- 1 pound ground turkey
- 1 tablespoon fresh mint leaves, finely chopped
- 1 teaspoon onion powder
- 1 ½ teaspoons garlic paste

- 1 teaspoon crushed red pepper flakes
- 1/4 cup melted butter
- 3/4 teaspoon fine sea salt
- 1/4 cup grated Pecorino Romano

Directions

1. Simply place all of the above ingredients into the mixing dish; mix until everything is well incorporated.

2. Use an ice cream scoop to shape the meat into golf ball sized meatballs.

3. Air fry the meatballs at 380 degrees F for approximately 7 minutes; work in batches, shaking them to ensure evenness of cooking.

4. Serve with simple tomato sauce garnished with fresh basil leaves. Bon appétit!

6 Servings

Ready in about
20 minutes

PER SERVING:
252 Calories; 15.9g Fat;
10.0g Carbs; 17.1g
Protein; 2.7g Sugars

Stuck on what to make for dinner? Treat your family to these restaurant-style, addictive turkey sliders. If you are short of time, just serve mayo and mustard instead of preparing the chive mayo. Easy!

Ingredients

For the Turkey Sliders:

- 3/4 pound turkey mince
- 1/4 cup pickled jalapeno, chopped
- 1 tablespoon oyster sauce
- 1-2 cloves garlic, minced
- 1 tablespoon chopped fresh cilantro
- 2 tablespoons chopped scallions
- Sea salt and ground black pepper, to savor

For the Chive Mayo:

- 1 cup mayonnaise
- 1 tablespoon chives
- 1 teaspoon salt
- Zest of 1 lime

Directions

1. In a mixing bowl, thoroughly combine all ingredients for the turkey sliders.

2. Mold the mixture into 6 even-sized slider patties. Then, air-fry them at 365 degrees F for 15 minutes.

3. Meanwhile, make the Chive Mayo by mixing the rest of the above ingredients. Assemble the sandwiches with burger buns and serve warm.

33. HONEY-GLAZED THANKSGIVING TURKEY BREAST

6 Servings

Ready in about
55 minutes

PER SERVING:
386 Calories; 8.2g Fat;
24.5g Carbs; 51.7g
Protein; 22.2g Sugars

A tasty holiday main dish that has all the best flavors of the season, prepared with ingredients your family and guests would love. Enjoy!

Ingredients

- 2 teaspoons butter, softened
- 1 teaspoon dried sage
- 2 sprigs rosemary, chopped
- 1 teaspoon salt
- 1/4 teaspoon freshly ground black pepper, or more to taste

- 1 whole turkey breast
- 2 tablespoons turkey broth
- 1/4 cup honey
- 2 tablespoons whole-grain mustard
- 1 tablespoon butter

Directions

1. Start by preheating your Air Fryer to 360 degrees F.

2. To make the rub, combine 2 tablespoons of butter, sage, rosemary, salt, and pepper; mix well to combine and spread it evenly over the surface of the turkey breast.

3. Roast for 20 minutes in an Air Fryer cooking basket. Flip the turkey breast over and cook for a further 15 to 16 minutes. Now, flip it back over and roast for 12 minutes more.

4. While the turkey is roasting, whisk the other ingredients in a saucepan. After that, spread the glaze all over the turkey breast.

5. Return to the Air Fryer for another 5 minutes; let the turkey rest for a few minutes before carving. Bon appétit!

34. CROWD-PLEASING TURKEY AND QUINOA SKEWERS

8 Servings

Ready in about
15 minutes

PER SERVING:
236 Calories; 12.1g
Fat; 15.6g Carbs; 18.2g
Protein; 0.0g Sugars

These great meatballs get a nutrition boost from amazing quinoa that is one of the healthiest foods on the Earth. Quinoa is packed with vitamins, minerals, useful fiber, protein, etc.

Ingredients

- 1 cup red quinoa, cooked
- 1 ½ cups of water
- 14 ounces ground turkey
- 2 small eggs, beaten
- 1 teaspoon ground ginger
- 2 ½ tablespoons vegetable oil

- 1 cup chopped fresh parsley
- 2 tablespoons seasoned breadcrumbs
- 3/4 teaspoon salt
- 1 heaping teaspoon fresh rosemary, finely chopped
- 1/2 teaspoon ground allspice

Directions

1. Mix all of the above ingredients in a bowl. Knead the mixture with your hands.

2. Then, take small portions and gently roll them into balls.

3. Now, preheat your Air Fryer to 380 degrees F. Air fry for 8 to 10 minutes in the Air Fryer basket. Serve on a serving platter with skewers and eat with your favorite dipping sauce.

35. HOLIDAY COLBY TURKEY MEATLOAF

6 Servings

Ready in about
50 minutes

PER SERVING:
252 Calories; 11.5g Fat;
8.7g Carbs; 27.5g Protein;
3.2g Sugars

Soft, moist meatloaf that is loaded with fragrant herbs and cheese. Keep in mind that Colby cheese is a perfect match for turkey but you can use another semi-hard cheese as needed.

Ingredients

- 1 pound turkey mince
- 1/2 cup scallions, finely chopped
- 2 garlic cloves, finely minced
- 1 teaspoon dried thyme
- 1/2 teaspoon dried basil
- 3/4 cup Colby cheese, shredded
- 3/4 cup crushed saltines

- 1 tablespoon tamari sauce
- Salt and black pepper, to your liking
- 1/4 cup roasted red pepper tomato sauce
- 1 teaspoon brown sugar
- 3/4 tablespoons olive oil
- 1 medium-sized egg, well beaten

Directions

1. In a nonstick skillet, that is preheated over a moderate heat, sauté the turkey mince, scallions, garlic, thyme, and basil until just tender and fragrant.

2. Then set your Air Fryer to cook at 360 degrees. Combine sautéed mixture with the cheese, saltines and tamari sauce; then form the mixture into a loaf shape.

3. Mix the remaining items and pour them over the meatloaf. Cook in the Air Fryer baking pan for 45 to 47 minutes. Eat warm.

4 Servings

Ready in about
40 minutes

PER SERVING:
413 Calories; 27.2g
Fat; 22.6g Carbs; 19.0g
Protein; 3.9g Sugars

Sweet Italian turkey sausages are combined with a mild mix of spices in this colorful, delicious recipe. Keep in mind that you can swap Sweet Italian turkey sausage for turkey sausage patties.

Ingredients

- 1 onion, cut into wedges
- 2 carrots, trimmed and sliced
- 1 parsnip, trimmed and sliced
- 2 potatoes, peeled and diced
- 1 teaspoon dried thyme
- 1/2 teaspoon dried marjoram

- 1 teaspoon dried basil
- 1/2 teaspoon celery seeds
- Sea salt and ground black pepper, to taste
- 1 tablespoon melted butter
- 3/4 pound sweet Italian turkey sausage

Directions

1. Mix the vegetables with all seasonings and melted butter. Arrange the vegetables on the bottom of the Air Fryer cooking basket. Lower the sausage onto the top of the vegetables.

2. Roast at 360 degrees F for 33 to 37 minutes or until the sausages are no longer pink. Work in batches as needed, shaking halfway through the roasting time. Bon appétit!

4 Servings

Ready in about
1 hour

PER SERVING:
467 Calories; 25.4g
Fat; 20.7g Carbs; 43.1g
Protein; 12.2g Sugars

Turkey stuffed with a tangy filling of prunes, spices and butter – this tastes like a holiday! Just soak prunes in water to make them soft before cutting. Enjoy!

Ingredients

- 3/4 cup prunes, pitted and chopped
- 1/2 teaspoon dried marjoram
- 1 sprig thyme, leaves only, crushed
- 2 tablespoons fresh coriander, minced

- 1/4 teaspoon ground allspice
- 1/2 cup softened butter
- 1 ½ pounds turkey tenderloins
- 2 tablespoons dry white wine

Directions

1. In a mixing bowl, thoroughly combine the first 6 ingredients; stir with a spoon until everything is well shared.

2. Cut the "pockets" into the sides of the turkey tenderloins. Stuff them with prepared prune mixture. Now, tie each "pocket" with a cooking twine. Sprinkle them with white wine.

3. Cook the stuffed turkey in the preheated Air Fryer at 385 degrees F for 48 to 55 minutes, checking periodically.

4. Afterward, remove cooking twine, cut each turkey tenderloin into 2 slices and serve immediately.

4 Servings

Ready in about
30 minutes

PER SERVING:
384 Calories; 22.6g
Fat; 27.6g Carbs; 21.7g
Protein; 8.5g Sugars

These peppers are full of rich, old-fashioned flavor, reminding us of grandma's cooking. Try to use the peppers of different colors to express your artistic side!

Ingredients

- 1/4 cup canola oil
- 7 ounces ground turkey
- 1/2 cup onion, finely chopped
- 2 cloves garlic, peeled and finely minced
- 1/2 cup quinoa, cooked
- 1 tablespoon fresh cilantro, chopped
- 1 tablespoon fresh parsley, chopped

- 1 ½ cups chopped tomatoes
- 1 teaspoon dried basil
- Salt and black pepper, to taste
- 4 bell peppers, slice off the tops, deveined
- 1/2 cup fat-free chicken broth
- 1 tablespoon cider vinegar
- 1/3 cup shredded three-cheese blend

Directions

1. Preheat the oil in a saucepan over a moderate heat. Now, sauté the turkey, onion and garlic for 4 to 5 minutes or until they have softened.

2. Add cooked quinoa, cilantro, parsley, 1 cup of tomatoes, basil, salt, and black pepper.

3. Stuff the peppers with the prepared meat filling. Transfer them to a baking dish.

4. After that, thoroughly combine the remaining tomatoes with chicken broth and cider vinegar. Add the sauce to the baking dish.

5. Cook covered at 360 degrees F for 18 minutes. Uncover, top with cheese and cook for 5 minutes more or until cheese is bubbling. Serve right away.

4 Servings

Ready in about
20 minutes

PER SERVING:
240 Calories; 2.6g Fat;
28.2g Carbs; 27.1g
Protein; 4.6g Sugars

Turkey fingers are one of our greatest guilty pleasures. These ones aren't deep-fried so you can relax and enjoy them to the fullest. Cajun spice mix makes them irresistible!

Ingredients

- 1/2 cup cornmeal mix
- 1/2 cup all-purpose flour
- 1 ½ tablespoons Cajun seasoning
- 1 ½ tablespoons whole-grain mustard
- 1 ½ cups buttermilk

- 1 teaspoon soy sauce
- 3/4 pound turkey tenderloins, cut into finger-sized strips
- Salt and ground black pepper, to your liking

Directions

1. Grab three bowls. Combine the cornmeal, flour, and Cajun seasoning in the first bowl. Mix the whole-grain mustard, buttermilk and soy sauce in the second one.

2. Season the turkey fingers with the salt and black pepper. Now, dip each strip into the buttermilk mix; after that, cover them with the cornmeal mixture on all sides.

3. Transfer the prepared turkey fingers to the Air Fryer baking pan and cook for 15 minutes at 360 degrees F. Serve with hot tomato ketchup and enjoy!

40. MUST-SERVE ROASTED TURKEY THIGHS WITH VEGETABLES

4 Servings

Ready in about
1 hour 15 minutes

PER SERVING:
218 Calories; 5.6g Fat;
8.7g Carbs; 31.9g Protein;
4.0g Sugars

Roasted turkey thighs with vegetables are a fantastic alternative to cooking a whole bird for Christmas or Thanksgiving. Keep it simple and save your time in the kitchen. You deserve it!

Ingredients

- 1 red onion, cut into wedges
- 1 carrot, trimmed and sliced
- 1 celery stalk, trimmed and sliced
- 1 cup Brussel sprouts, trimmed and halved
- 1 cup roasted vegetable broth
- 1 tablespoon apple cider vinegar
- 1 teaspoon maple syrup
- 2 turkey thighs

- 1/2 teaspoon mixed peppercorns, freshly cracked
- 1 teaspoon fine sea salt
- 1 teaspoon cayenne pepper
- 1 teaspoon onion powder
- 1/2 teaspoon garlic powder
- 1/3 teaspoon mustard seeds

Directions

1. Take a baking dish that easily fits into your device; place the vegetables on the bottom of the baking dish and pour in roasted vegetable broth.

2. In a large-sized mixing dish, place the remaining ingredients; let them marinate for about 30 minutes. Lay them on the top of the vegetables.

3. Roast at 330 degrees F for 40 to 45 minutes. Bon appétit!

Air Fryer Cookbook | Turkey

41. HOT PEPPERY TURKEY SANDWICHES

4 Servings

Ready in about
25 minutes

PER SERVING:
207 Calories; 8.7g Fat;
19.9g Carbs; 13.5g
Protein; 4.2g Sugars

This Air Fryer recipe is a great way to use leftover turkey. Combine it with your favorite vegetables, serve in hamburger buns and you will have a delicious dinner. It freezes well, too.

Ingredients

- 1 cup leftover turkey, cut into bite-sized chunks
- 2 bell peppers, deveined and chopped
- 1 Serrano pepper, deveined and chopped
- 1 leek, sliced
- 1/2 cup sour cream
- 1 teaspoon hot paprika

- 3/4 teaspoon kosher salt
- 1/2 teaspoon ground black pepper
- 1 heaping tablespoon fresh cilantro, chopped
- A few dashes of Tabasco sauce
- 4 hamburger buns

Directions

1. Toss all ingredients, without the hamburger buns, in an Air Fryer baking pan; toss until everything is well coated.

2. Now, roast it for 20 minutes at 385 degrees F. Serve on hamburger buns; add some extra sour cream and Dijon mustard if desired. Bon appétit!

42. HOISIN-GLAZED TURKEY DRUMSTICKS

4 Servings

Ready in about
20 minutes +
marinating time

PER SERVING:
397 Calories; 18.5g Fat;
9.6g Carbs; 44.3g Protein;
7.3g Sugars

Hoisin sauce is commonly used as a glaze for meat because of its thick texture.
Add some mustard and honey and you will get a perfect glaze for your festive meat
main course.

Ingredients

- 2 turkey drumsticks
- 2 tablespoons balsamic vinegar
- 2 tablespoons dry white wine
- 1 tablespoon extra-virgin olive oil
- 1 sprig rosemary, chopped
- Salt and ground black pepper, to your liking
- 2 ½ tablespoons butter, melted

For the Hoisin Glaze:

- 2 tablespoons hoisin sauce
- 1 tablespoon honey
- 1 tablespoon honey mustard

Directions

1. Add the turkey drumsticks to a mixing dish; add the vinegar, wine, olive oil, and rosemary. Let them marinate for 3 hours.

2. Then, preheat the Air Fryer to 350 degrees F.

3. Season the turkey drumsticks with salt and black pepper; spread the melted butter over the surface of drumsticks.

4. Cook turkey drumsticks at 350 degrees F for 30 to 35 minutes, working in batches. Turn the drumsticks over a few times during the cooking.

5. While the turkey drumsticks are roasting, prepare the Hoisin glaze by mixing all the glaze ingredients. After that, drizzle the turkey with the glaze mixture; roast for a further 5 minutes. Let it rest about 10 minutes before carving and serving. Bon appétit!

43. THAI STICKY TURKEY WINGS

4 Servings

Ready in about
40 minutes

PER SERVING:
284 Calories; 14.1g
Fat; 18.8g Carbs; 19.4g
Protein; 13.9g Sugars

Try this recipe and you will find that air-frying is one of the best ways to make perfect sticky wings. Use a few dashes of Tabasco sauce for spicier wings.

Ingredients

- 3/4 pound turkey wings, cut into pieces
- 1 teaspoon ginger powder
- 1 teaspoon garlic powder
- 3/4 teaspoon paprika
- 2 tablespoons soy sauce
- 1 handful minced lemongrass

- Sea salt flakes and ground black pepper, to savor
- 2 tablespoons rice wine vinegar
- 1/4 cup peanut butter
- 1 tablespoon sesame oil
- 1/2 cup Thai sweet chili sauce

Directions

1. In a saucepan with boiling water, cook the turkey wings for 20 minutes.

2. Transfer the turkey wings to a large-sized mixing dish; toss with the remaining ingredients, without Thai sweet chili sauce.

3. Air-fry them for 20 minutes at 350 degrees F or until they are thoroughly cooked; make sure to flip them over during the cooking time.

4. Serve with Thai sweet chili sauce and lemon wedges. Bon appétit!

44. FINGER-LICKIN' VERMOUTH AND HONEY TURKEY

4 Servings

Ready in about
55 minutes +
marinating time

PER SERVING:
256 Calories; 9.2g Fat;
5.4g Carbs; 33.4g Protein;
4.7g Sugars

Marinated turkey tenderloin is delicious any time of the year. Serve with sautéed Brussels sprouts and a glass of rosé wine. Enjoy!

Ingredients

- 1 teaspoon marjoram
- 1 teaspoon dried oregano
- 1 tablespoon honey
- 1/4 cup vermouth
- 2 tablespoons lemon juice
- 1 turkey tenderloin, quartered

- 1 tablespoon sesame oil
- Sea salt flakes, to savor
- 1/2 teaspoon freshly ground pepper, or to savor
- 3/4 teaspoon smoked paprika
- 1 teaspoon crushed sage leaves, dried

Directions

1. Place the first 6 ingredients in a mixing dish; let it marinate for 3 hours at least.

2. Then, drizzle the turkey breasts with sesame oil and add the other ingredients.

3. Lastly, roast in the Air Fryer cooking basket about 50 to 55 minutes at 355 degrees F; make sure to turn them over a few times during the cooking time.

45. SPICED SCALLION STUFFED TURKEY ROULADE

4 Servings

Ready in about
50 minutes

PER SERVING:
227 Calories; 10.8g Fat;
1.5g Carbs; 29.7g Protein;
0.0g Sugars

A meat roulade is always a good idea for an elegant party dinner but you can't go wrong if you serve it for any occasion.

Ingredients

- 1 turkey fillet
- Salt and garlic pepper, to your liking
- 1/3 teaspoon onion powder
- 1/2 teaspoon dried basil
- 1/3 teaspoon ground red chipotle pepper
- 1 ½ teaspoons mustard seeds

- 1/2 teaspoon fennel seeds
- 2 tablespoons melted butter
- 3 tablespoons coriander, finely chopped
- 1/2 cup scallions, finely chopped
- 2 clove garlic, finely minced

Directions

1. Place the turkey fillets on a clean and dry surface. Then, flatten the fillets to a thickness of about 1/2-inch using a meat mallet. Sprinkle them with salt, garlic pepper, and onion powder.

2. Then, mix the basil, chipotle pepper, mustard seeds, fennel seeds and butter in a small-sized bowl. Spread this mixture over the fillets, leaving an inch border.

3. Top with coriander, scallions and garlic. Roll the fillets towards the border. Lastly, secure the rolls with a cooking twine and transfer them to the Air Fryer cooking basket.

4. Roast at 350 degrees F for about 50 minutes; turn it halfway through the roasting time. Check for doneness and serve warm.

PORK

50

55

60

58

46

8 Servings

Ready in about
50 minutes

PER SERVING:
428 Calories; 28.8g
Fat; 14.3g Carbs; 26.8g
Protein; 2.1g Sugars

For the most beautiful dinner parties, try these easy, puffy rolls that melt in your mouth. A feast for all senses!

Ingredients

- 1 (8-ounce) can crescent dinner rolls
- 1 heaping tablespoon fresh basil leaves, finely chopped
- 1 heaping tablespoon fresh parsley, finely chopped

- 1 (8-ounce) package smoked Gruyere cheese, grated
- 3/4 pound smoked bacon, coarsely chopped
- 1 medium-sized egg, well-beaten

Directions

1. Begin by preheating your Air Fryer to 325 degrees F.

2. Next, separate crescent dough into 8 triangles. Divide the fresh herbs among crescents and press them lightly into dough.

3. Then, add the cheese and the bacon. Roll up each crescent, starting at longest side. After that, firmly pinch edges to seal; brush them with the egg. Afterwards, gently stretch each crescent.

4. Transfer them to the Air Fryer basket and press the power button; bake about 7 minutes. Now, pause the machine, turn the temperature to 385 degrees F and cook for further 4 minutes. Eat warm.

47. AROMATIC PORK WITH ROOT VEGGIES

6 Servings

Ready in about
30 minutes

PER SERVING:
585 Calories; 30.7g
Fat; 14.1g Carbs; 53.9g
Protein; 2.0g Sugars

One of the favorite "fix-it-and-forget-it" recipes. Try to cut the meat and vegetables all the same size so that they can roast evenly.

Ingredients

- 1 ½ pounds pork belly
- 2 medium-sized carrots, cut into thick slices
- 2 Russet potatoes, peeled and diced
- 2 cloves garlic, finely minced
- 2 green onions, quartered, white and green parts
- 1/4 cup cooking wine
- Kosher salt and ground black pepper, to taste
- 1 teaspoon cayenne pepper
- 1 tablespoon coriander
- 1 teaspoon celery seeds

Directions

1. Blanch the pork belly in boiling water for approximately 15 minutes. Then, cut it into chunks.

2. Arrange the pork chunks, carrots, and potatoes in the Air Fryer basket. Add the minced garlic and green onions. Drizzle everything with cooking wine of your choice.

3. Sprinkle with salt, black pepper, cayenne pepper, fresh coriander, and celery seeds. Toss to coat well.

4. Roast in the preheated Air Fryer at 330 degrees F for 30 minutes.

5. Serve on individual serving plates. Bon appétit!

48. TANGY FRIED PORK BALLS

4 Servings

Ready in about
20 minutes

PER SERVING:
175 Calories; 4.1g Fat;
2.8g Carbs; 30.3g Protein;
0.6g Sugars

This is a new twist of an old-fashioned favorite. Just add a turmeric powder and fresh ginger to these balls for an ambrosial flavor and enjoy them submerged in your favorite sauce. Yummy!

Ingredients

- 1 pound ground pork
- 1 cup scallions, finely chopped
- 2 cloves garlic, finely minced
- 1 ½ tablespoons Worcester sauce
- 1 tablespoon oyster sauce

- 1 teaspoon turmeric powder
- 1/2 teaspoon freshly grated ginger root
- 1 tablespoon breadcrumbs
- 1 small sliced red chili, for garnish

Directions

1. Mix all of the above ingredients, apart from the red chili. Knead with your hands to ensure an even mixture.

2. Roll into equal balls and transfer them to the Air Fryer cooking basket.

3. Set the timer for 15 minutes and push the power button. Air-fry at 350 degrees F. Sprinkle with sliced red chili; serve immediately with your favorite sauce for dipping. Enjoy!

49. RICH FILLED MEXICAN WRAPS

10 Servings

Ready in about
20 minutes

PER SERVING:
314 Calories; 7.5g Fat;
40.4g Carbs; 19.7g
Protein; 2.3g Sugars

This life-changing bites can be served as an amazing dinner or tempting snacks.
Don't replace Mexican cheese blend in order to perfect your wraps.

Ingredients

- 1/4 pound ground pork
- 1/2 pound ground beef
- 2 rashers bacon
- 1 ½ teaspoons Mexican spice mix
- 1 ounce tomato ketchup

- 9 ounces canned crushed tomatoes, drained
- 1 chipotle pepper, deveined and chopped
- 20 wonton wrappers
- 3/4 cup Mexican cheese blend, fine cut shredded

Directions

1. In a large-sized skillet that is preheated over a moderate flame, brown the pork, beef and the bacon. Then, using a spatula, crumble the browned meat and crush the bacon; then drain.

2. Stir in Mexican spice mix, ketchup, crushed tomatoes, and chipotle pepper.

3. Lightly grease a mini muffin tin with a pan spray; add wonton wrappers to the muffin tin and press to form the cups. Fill them with the meat mixture; top each cup with cheese.

4. Bake in the preheated device at 360 degrees F approximately 11 minutes. Bon appétit!

50. GRANDMA'S GARLICKY PORK TENDERLOIN

4 Servings

Ready in about
20 minutes +
marinating time

PER SERVING:
168 Calories; 4.1g Fat;
1.4g Carbs; 29.9g Protein;
0.0g Sugars

Flavorsome pork with garlic and fragrant herbs – just like grandma used to make it!
To tuck garlic slivers into the slits, you can also score the meat i.e. cut small slits in
a criss-cross pattern.

Ingredients

- 1 pound pork tenderloin
- 4-5 garlic cloves, peeled and halved
- 1 teaspoon kosher salt
- 1/3 teaspoon ground black pepper
- 1 teaspoon dried basil

- 1/2 teaspoon dried oregano
- 1/2 teaspoon dried rosemary
- 1/2 teaspoon dried marjoram
- 2 tablespoons cooking wine

Directions

1. Rub the pork with garlic halves; add the seasoning and drizzle with the cooking wine. Then, cut slits completely through pork tenderloin. Tuck the remaining garlic into the slits.

2. Wrap the pork tenderloin with foil; let it marinate overnight.

3. Roast at 360 degrees F for 15 to 17 minutes. Serve warm with roasted potatoes. Bon appétit!

6 Servings

Ready in about
50 minutes

This is very simple but delicious weeknight meal. Soaking the strips into a marinade only for half an hour will make them tender. After that, they need to be fried for 7 to 8 minutes.

Ingredients

- 1 pound boneless center-cut loin pork chops, cut into 1/2-inch strips
- 2 tablespoons bourbon
- 1 teaspoon honey
- 1/2 teaspoon chili powder
- 1 teaspoon celery seeds

- 1/2 teaspoon mustard seeds
- 1 teaspoon peeled fresh ginger, freshly grated
- Salt and freshly ground black pepper, to your liking
- 1/2 cup all-purpose flour
- 6 ounces seasoned breadcrumbs

Directions

1. Place the pork strips together with the bourbon, honey, chili powder, celery seeds, mustard seeds and the ginger in a zip-top plastic bag; seal and place in your refrigerator 30 to 45 minutes.

2. After that, remove the pork from the marinade and season with salt and pepper. Coat with flour and finally dip it into the breadcrumbs.

3. Set your Air Fryer to cook at 380 degrees F. Press the power button and air-fry for 4 minutes; pause the machine, shake the basket and cook for 3 more minutes.

4. Serve with warm rice noodles.

52. SUNDAY PORK ROAST

6 Servings

Ready in about
55 minutes

PER SERVING:
278 Calories; 16.0g Fat;
0.3g Carbs; 31.2g Protein;
0.0g Sugars

If you are lucky enough to own an Air Fryer, then, you can prepare your Sunday pork roast in the easiest possible way. To serve it up, add wild rice to each serving plate. Ta-Da! Delight your family and guests!

Ingredients

- 1 ½ pounds boneless pork loin roast, washed
- 1 teaspoon mustard seeds
- 1 teaspoon garlic powder
- 1 teaspoon porcini powder

- 1 teaspoon shallot powder
- 3/4 teaspoon sea salt flakes
- 1 teaspoon red pepper flakes, crushed
- 2 dried sprigs thyme, crushed
- 2 tablespoons lime juice

Directions

1. Firstly, score the meat using a small knife; make sure to not cut too deep.

2. In a small-sized mixing dish, combine all seasonings in the order listed above; mix to combine well.

3. Massage the spice mix into the pork meat to evenly distribute. Drizzle with lemon juice.

4. Then, set your Air Fryer to cook at 360 degrees F. Place the pork in the Air Fryer basket; roast for 25 to 30 minutes. Pause the machine, check for doneness and cook for 25 minutes more.

53. MARJORAM TORTILLA BURGERS WITH MINT DIP

4 Servings

Ready in about
40 minutes

PER SERVING:
302 Calories; 10.8g
Fat; 15.7g Carbs; 34.8g
Protein; 1.5g Sugars

These tortillas stand out from all the others thanks to a tangy mint spread, aromatic marjoram, and flavorsome pork mince. Don't forget to microwave your tortillas before serving!

Ingredients

For the Pork Sliders:

- 1 pound pork, ground
- 1 onion, peeled and finely chopped
- 2 garlic cloves, minced
- 1 ½ teaspoons whole-grain mustard
- Salt and ground black pepper, to taste
- 1/2 teaspoon cumin powder
- 1 tablespoon marjoram
- 1/4 cup Gruyère cheese, shredded

For the Mint Spread:

- 1/4 cup sour cream
- 1/4 soft cheese
- 1/4 cup fresh mint, coarsely chopped
- 4 whole-wheat tortillas

Directions

1. Thoroughly combine all the ingredients for the pork balls; knead with your hands for better results.

2. Shape into 4 patties. Air-fry for 35 to 40 minutes at 370 degrees, cooking in batches. Make sure to flip them over halfway through the cooking time.

3. While the sliders are cooking, combine the sour cream with soft cheese and mint leaves.

4. Then, warm and soften the tortillas in the microwave; divide the mint spread among tortillas. Add cooked pork sliders and serve immediately.

54. FLAVORSOME BARBECUE PORK CHOPS

6 Servings

Ready in about
20 minutes

PER SERVING:
285 Calories; 20.0g Fat;
6.2g Carbs; 18.8g Protein;
0.7g Sugars

In this recipe, you can marinate the chops with seasonings for about 3 hours or overnight; it will certainly add flavor. However, if you are short on time, don't worry; feel free to skip that step.

Ingredients

- 6 pork chops
- Hickory-smoked salt, to savor
- Ground black pepper, to savor
- 1 teaspoon onion powder
- 1/2 teaspoon garlic powder
- 1/2 teaspoon cayenne pepper
- 1 teaspoon packed brown sugar
- 1/3 cup all-purpose flour

Directions

1. Simply place all of the above ingredients into a zip-top plastic bag; shake them up to coat well.

2. Spritz the chops with a pan spray (canola spray works well here) and transfer them to the Air Fryer cooking basket.

3. Roast them for 20 minutes at 375 degrees F. Serve with sautéed vegetables. Bon appétit!

55. PARMESAN PORK SAUSAGE MEATBALLS

4 Servings

Ready in about
20 minutes

PER SERVING:
207 Calories; 11.1g
Fat; 16.6g Carbs; 10.1g
Protein; 4.3g Sugars

If you have only 20 minutes, you can easily cook these heavenly meatballs with a touch of Parmesan cheese with delightful marinara sauce. Sounds tasty? Okay, let's get cooking!

Ingredients

- 1 cup pork sausage meat
- 1 shallot, finely chopped
- 2 garlic cloves, finely minced
- 1/2 teaspoon fine sea salt
- 1/4 teaspoon ground black pepper, or more to taste

- 3/4 teaspoon paprika
- 1 ½ tablespoons parmesan cheese, preferably freshly grated
- 1/2 cup seasoned breadcrumbs
- 1/2 jar marinara sauce

Directions

1. Mix all of the above ingredients, except the marinara sauce, in a large-sized dish, until everything is well incorporated.

2. Shape into meatballs. Air-fry them at 360 degrees F for 10 minutes; pause the Air Fryer, shake them up and cook for additional 6 minutes or until the balls are no longer pink in the middle.

3. Meanwhile, heat the marinara sauce over a medium flame. Serve the pork sausage meatballs with marinara sauce. Bon appétit!

56. PORK SLICES WITH CORIANDER-GARLIC SAUCE

4 Servings

Ready in about
30 minutes +
marinating time

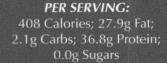

PER SERVING:
408 Calories; 27.9g Fat;
2.1g Carbs; 36.8g Protein;
0.0g Sugars

Pork slices with crispy crackling are a culinary version of the little black dress!
Air-frying is one of the best ways to achieve this extraordinary, vivid impression.

Ingredients

- 1 pound pork butt, cut into pieces 2-inches long
- 1 teaspoon cornstarch
- 1 egg white, well whisked
- Salt and ground black pepper, to taste
- 1 tablespoon olive oil
- 1 tablespoon soy sauce
- 1 teaspoon lemon juice, preferably freshly squeezed

For the Coriander-Garlic Sauce:

- 3 garlic cloves, peeled
- 1/3 cup fresh parsley leaves
- 1/3 cup fresh coriander leaves
- 1/2 tablespoon salt
- 1 teaspoon lemon juice
- 1/3 cup extra-virgin olive oil

Directions

1. Combine the pork strips with cornstarch, egg white, salt, pepper, olive oil, soy sauce, and lemon juice. Cover and refrigerate for 30 to 45 minutes.

2. After that, spritz the pork strips with a nonstick cooking spray.

3. Set your Air Fryer to cook at 380 degrees F. Press the power button and air-fry for 15 minutes; pause the machine, shake the basket and cook for 15 more minutes.

4. Meanwhile, puree the garlic in a food processor until finely minced. Now, puree the parsley, coriander, salt, and lemon juice. With the machine running, carefully pour in the olive oil.

5. Serve chilled sauce with pork slices and enjoy!

4 Servings

Ready in about
15 minutes +
marinating time

PER SERVING:
438 Calories; 27.3g Fat;
3.8g Carbs; 32.2g Protein;
1.5g Sugars

Pork ribs in classic red wine sauce – it smells like holiday happiness! This classic sauce will improve the flavor and presentation of the pork ribs.

Ingredients

For the Pork Ribs:

- 1 pound pork ribs
- 2 tablespoons olive oil
- 1/2 teaspoon freshly cracked black peppercorns
- 1/2 teaspoon Hickory-smoked salt
- 1 tablespoon Dijon honey mustard
- 1/4 cup soy sauce
- 1 clove garlic, minced

For the Red Wine Sauce:

- 1 ½ cups beef stock
- 1 cup red wine
- 1 teaspoon brown sugar
- 1 teaspoon balsamic vinegar
- 1/4 teaspoon salt

Directions

1. Place all ingredients for the pork ribs in a large-sized mixing dish. Cover and marinate in your refrigerator overnight or at least 3 hours.

2. Air-fry the pork ribs for 10 minutes at 320 degrees F.

3. Meanwhile, make the sauce. Add a beef stock to a deep pan that is preheated over a moderate flame; boil until it is reduced by half.

4. Add the remaining ingredients and increase the temperature to high heat. Let it cook for further 10 minutes or until your sauce is reduced by half.

5. Serve the pork ribs with red wine sauce. Bon appétit!

58. GRILLED SAGE RACK OF PORK

4 Servings

Ready in about 15 minutes + marinating time

PER SERVING:
295 Calories; 4.2g Fat; 32.5g Carbs; 30.2g Protein; 25.9g Sugars

An elegant entrée for a special dinner. Serve with buttered green beans, Waldorf salad, dinner rolls and rose wine.

Ingredients

- 1 rib rack of pork, chine bone cut off
- 1 teaspoon shallot powder
- 1/2 teaspoon cumin powder
- 2 gloves garlic, finely minced
- Salt and pepper, to your liking

- 1 ½ tablespoons Teriyaki sauce
- 1 cup BBQ sauce
- 2 tablespoons honey
- 1 heaping tablespoon fresh sage, snipped

Directions

1. Put all the ingredients, except the fresh sage leaves, into a mixing dish; let it marinate for at least 30 minutes.

2. Then, set your Air Fryer to cook at 360 degrees F; air-fry the marinated pork using the Air Fryer grill pan for 15 minutes. Check for doneness and serve sprinkled with snipped fresh sage.

59. CLASSIC ROSEMARY PORK MEATLOAF

6 Servings

Ready in about
30 minutes

PER SERVING:
282 Calories; 19.2g Fat;
9.2g Carbs; 18.3g Protein;
5.1g Sugars

Spicy pork sausage and ground turkey with aromatic rosemary, make this a sumptuous meal for any occasion! What about leftovers? Try to make the sandwiches; just add a crisp lettuce and pickled red onions, and enjoy!

Ingredients

- Non-stick cooking spray
- 1 shallot, finely chopped
- 1 rib celery, finely chopped
- 2 gloves garlic, minced
- 1 tablespoon Worcestershire sauce
- 3/4 pound spicy ground pork sausage
- 1/4 pound ground turkey

- 2 sprigs rosemary, leaves only, crushed
- 1/4 cup minced fresh parsley
- 1 egg, lightly whisked
- 3 tablespoons fresh panko
- Salt and freshly ground pepper, to your liking
- 1/3 cup tomato ketchup

Directions

1. Spritz a cast-iron skillet with a cooking spray. Then, sauté the shallots, celery and garlic until just tender and fragrant.

2. Now, add Worcestershire sauce and both kinds of meat to the sautéed mixture. Remove from the heat. Add the rosemary, parsley, egg, fresh panko, salt, and pepper; mix to combine well.

3. Transfer the mixture to the baking pan and shape into a loaf. Cover the prepared meatloaf with tomato ketchup.

4. Air-fry at 390 degrees F for 25 minutes or until thoroughly warmed.

60. THREE-PEPPER ROAST PORK LOIN

6 Servings

Ready in about
30 minutes

PER SERVING:
241 Calories; 14.4g Fat;
5.3g Carbs; 22.2g Protein;
3.3g Sugars

The key to this sophisticated roast – cut slits to hold the chunks of peppers and massage the seasoning into the meat. You'll thank us later.

Ingredients

- 1 tablespoon olive oil
- 1 pound pork loin
- 1 teaspoon dried basil
- 1/2 teaspoon dried oregano
- 1/4 teaspoon crushed red pepper flakes
- 1 teaspoon dried thyme
- 1/4 teaspoon freshly grated nutmeg
- Sea salt flakes and freshly ground black pepper, to taste

- 1 Pimento chili pepper, deveined and chopped
- 1 Yellow wax pepper, deveined and chopped
- 1 sweet bell pepper, deveined and chopped
- 1 tablespoon peanut butter
- 1/4 cup beef broth
- 1/2 tablespoon whole-grain mustard
- 1 bay leaf

Directions

1. Lightly grease the inside of an Air Fryer baking dish with a thin layer of olive oil. Then, cut 8 slit down the center of pork (about 3x3"). Sprinkle with the seasonings and massage them into the meat to evenly distribute

2. Then, tuck peppers into the slits and transfer the meat to the Air Fryer baking dish. Scatter remaining peppers around the roast.

3. In a mixing dish, whisk the peanut butter, beef broth, and mustard; now, pour broth mixture around the roast.

4. Add the bay leaf and roast the meat for 25 minutes at 390 degrees F; turn the pork over halfway through the roasting time. Bon appétit!

BEEF

62

71

68

74

65

4 Servings

Ready in about
20 minutes

PER SERVING:
167 Calories; 5.5g Fat;
1.4g Carbs; 26.4g Protein;
0.0g Sugars

This recipe looks like the American classic but it is inspired by Asian soy sauce and fresh scallions. Serve with spicy homemade sauce and enjoy!

Ingredients

- 3/4 pound lean ground beef
- 1 tablespoon soy sauce
- 1 teaspoon Dijon mustard
- A few dashes of liquid smoke
- 1 teaspoon shallot powder
- 1 clove garlic, minced
- 1/2 teaspoon cumin powder

- 1/4 cup scallions, minced
- 1/3 teaspoon sea salt flakes
- 1/3 teaspoon freshly cracked mixed peppercorns
- 1 teaspoon celery seeds
- 1 teaspoon parsley flakes

Directions

1. Mix all of the above ingredients in a bowl; knead until everything is well incorporated.

2. Shape the mixture into four patties. Next, make a shallow dip in the center of each patty to prevent them puffing up during air-frying.

3. Spritz the patties on all sides using a non-stick cooking spray. Cook approximately 12 minutes at 360 degrees F. Check for doneness – an instant read thermometer should read 160 degrees F. Serve them on butter rolls with toppings of choice. Bon appétit!

62. CHRISTMAS SMOKED BEEF ROAST

8 Servings

Ready in about
45 minutes

PER SERVING:
243 Calories; 10.6g Fat;
0.4g Carbs; 34.5g Protein;
0.0g Sugars

If you probably already know, the beef roast can be a tough meat if it is not cooked properly. Air-frying in one of the best ways to cook a moist and tender beef. Give it a try!

Ingredients

- 2 pounds roast beef, at room temperature
- 2 tablespoons extra-virgin olive oil
- 1 teaspoon sea salt flakes
- 1 teaspoon black pepper, preferably freshly ground

- 1 teaspoon smoked paprika
- A few dashes of liquid smoke
- 2 jalapeño peppers, thinly sliced

Directions

1. Start by preheating the Air Fryer to 330 degrees F.

2. Then, pat the roast dry using kitchen towels. Rub with extra-virgin olive oil and all seasonings along with liquid smoke.

3. Roast for 30 minutes in the preheated Air Fryer; then, pause the machine and turn the roast over; roast for additional 15 minutes.

4. Check for doneness using a meat thermometer and serve sprinkled with sliced jalapeños. Bon appétit!

63. COUNTRY-STYLE BEEF MEATLOAF

4 Servings

Ready in about
30 minutes

PER SERVING:
206 Calories; 7.9g Fat;
15.9g Carbs; 17.6g
Protein; 0.8g Sugars

The elusive flavor in this meatloaf comes from the seasonings and their zesty touch. It is important to add eggs and plain milk, which keep it moist and gooey.

Ingredients

- 3/4 pound ground chuck
- 1/4 pound ground pork sausage
- 1 cup shallot, finely chopped
- 2 eggs, well beaten
- 3 tablespoons plain milk
- 1 tablespoon oyster sauce
- 1 teaspoon porcini mushrooms

- 1/2 teaspoon cumin powder
- 1 teaspoon garlic paste
- 1 tablespoon fresh parsley
- Seasoned salt and crushed red pepper flakes, to taste
- 1 cup crushed saltines

Directions

1. Simply place all ingredients in a large-sized mixing dish; mix until everything is thoroughly combined.

2. Press the meatloaf mixture into the Air Fryer baking dish; set your Air Fryer to cook at 360 degrees F for 25 minutes. Press the power button and cook until heated through.

3. Check for doneness and serve with your favorite wine!

64. JAPANESE-STYLE MARINATED FLANK STEAK

4 Servings

Ready in about
15 minutes

PER SERVING:
367 Calories; 15.1g Fat;
6.4g Carbs; 48.6g Protein;
3.4g Sugars

This amazing Japanese-style marinade will enhance flavor and tenderize the meat.
It makes meat slightly springy and so tender!

Ingredients

- 3/4 pound flank steak
- 1 ½ tablespoons sake
- 1 tablespoon brown miso paste

- 1 teaspoon honey
- 2 garlic cloves, pressed
- 1 tablespoon olive oil

Directions

1. Place all the ingredients in a sealable food bag; shake until completely coated and place in your refrigerator for at least 1 hour.

2. Then, spritz the steak with a non-stick cooking spray; make sure to coat on all sides. Place the steak in the Air Fryer baking pan.

3. Set your Air Fryer to cook at 400 degrees F. Roast for 12 minutes, flipping twice. Serve immediately.

65. DINNER CIABATTA CHEESEBURGERS

4 Servings

Ready in about
15 minutes

PER SERVING:
271 Calories; 13.3g
Fat; 21.9g Carbs; 15.3g
Protein; 2.9g Sugars

Here are the decadent and flavorsome burgers… mmmm! Everybody loves comfort food but burgers will always have their special place in our hearts.

Ingredients

- 3/4 pound ground chuck
- 1 envelope onion soup mix
- Kosher salt and freshly ground black pepper, to taste

- 1 teaspoon paprika
- 4 slices Monterey-Jack cheese
- 4 ciabatta rolls
- Mustard and pickled salad, to serve

Directions

1. In a mixing dish, thoroughly combine ground chuck, onion soup mix, salt, black pepper, and paprika.

2. Then, set your Air Fryer to cook at 385 degrees F. Shape the mixture into 4 patties. Air-fry them for 10 minutes.

3. Next step, place the slices of cheese on the top of the warm burgers. Air-fry one minute more.

4. Serve on ciabatta rolls garnished with mustard and pickled salad of choice. Bon appétit!

66. PERFECT THAI MEATBALLS

4 Servings

Ready in about
20 minutes

PER SERVING:
242 Calories; 10.5g Fat;
0.2g Carbs; 34.4g Protein;
0.0g Sugars

Finger-lickin' customizable meatballs! You can serve these bouncy meatballs as a main course with warm rice or egg noodles. You can also serve them as an appetizer with a dipping sauce.

Ingredients

- 1 pound ground beef
- 1 teaspoon red Thai curry paste
- 1/2 lime, rind and juice

- 1 teaspoon Chinese spice
- 2 teaspoons lemongrass, finely chopped
- 1 tablespoon sesame oil

Directions

1. Thoroughly combine all ingredients in a mixing dish.

2. Shape into 24 meatballs and place them into the Air Fryer cooking basket. Cook at 380 degrees F for 10 minutes; pause the machine and cook for a further 5 minutes, or until cooked through.

3. Serve accompanied by the dipping sauce. Bon appétit!

4 Servings

Ready in about
20 minutes

PER SERVING:
268 Calories; 14.5g Fat;
1.0g Carbs; 32.0g Protein;
0.0g Sugars

This crunchy filet mignon is sure to become your holiday favorite! You can also experiment with seasonings and create your unique recipe!

Ingredients

- 1/2 pound filet mignon
- Sea salt and ground black pepper, to your liking
- 1/2 teaspoon cayenne pepper
- 1 teaspoon dried basil

- 1 teaspoon dried rosemary
- 1 teaspoon dried thyme
- 1 tablespoon sesame oil
- 1 small-sized egg, well-whisked
- 1/2 cup seasoned breadcrumbs

Directions

1. Season the filet mignon with salt, black pepper, cayenne pepper, basil, rosemary, and thyme. Brush with sesame oil.

2. Put the egg in a shallow plate. Now, place the breadcrumbs in another plate.

3. Coat the filet mignon with the egg; then, lay it into the crumbs. Set your Air Fryer to cook at 360 degrees F.

4. Cook for 10 to 13 minutes or until golden. Serve with mixed salad leaves and enjoy!

68. THE BEST LONDON BROIL EVER

8 Servings

Ready in about
30 minutes +
marinating time

PER SERVING:
257 Calories; 9.2g Fat;
0.1g Carbs; 41.0g Protein;
0.4g Sugars

This is a great recipe for chilly winter days. Serve this mouthwatering London broil with German potato salad and enjoy with your family!

Ingredients

- 2 pounds London broil
- 3 large garlic cloves, minced
- 3 tablespoons balsamic vinegar
- 3 tablespoons whole-grain mustard

- 2 tablespoons olive oil
- Sea salt and ground black pepper, to taste
- 1/2 teaspoon dried hot red pepper flakes

Directions

1. Score both sides of the cleaned London broil.

2. Thoroughly combine the remaining ingredients; massage this mixture into the meat to coat it on all sides. Let it marinate for at least 3 hours.

3. Set the Air Fryer to cook at 400 degrees F; Then cook the London broil for 15 minutes. Flip it over and cook another 10 to 12 minutes. Bon appétit!

4 Servings

Ready in about
20 minutes

PER SERVING:
352 Calories; 20.8g
Fat; 10.0g Carbs; 29.8g
Protein; 1.4g Sugars

The key to this amazing hearty stew – use fresh leek and garlic! In this recipe, please skip the extra lean steak and choose the one with a bit more fat.

Ingredients

- 3/4 pound beef sirloin steak, cut into small-sized strips
- 1/4 cup balsamic vinegar
- 1 tablespoon brown mustard
- 2 tablespoons all-purpose flour
- 1 tablespoon butter
- 1 cup beef broth

- 1 cup leek, chopped
- 2 cloves garlic, crushed
- 1 teaspoon cayenne pepper
- Sea salt flakes and crushed red pepper, to taste
- 1 cup sour cream
- 2 ½ tablespoons tomato paste

Directions

1. Place the beef along with the balsamic vinegar and the mustard in a mixing dish; cover and marinate in your refrigerator for about 1 hour.

2. Then, coat the beef strips with the flour; butter the inside of a baking dish and put the beef into the dish.

3. Add the broth, leeks and garlic. Cook at 380 degrees for 8 minutes. Pause the machine and add the cayenne pepper, salt, red pepper, sour cream and tomato paste; cook for additional 7 minutes.

4. Check for doneness and serve with warm egg noodles, if desired. Bon appétit!

70. TENDER BEEF CHUCK WITH BRUSSELS SPROUTS

4 Servings

Ready in about
25 minutes +
marinating time

PER SERVING:
302 Calories; 14.2g Fat;
6.5g Carbs; 36.6g Protein;
1.6g Sugars

If you have to choose among thousands and thousands of beef recipes, you would probably choose this one. Why is it so? Keep on reading…

Ingredients

- 1 pound beef chuck shoulder steak
- 2 tablespoons vegetable oil
- 1 tablespoon red wine vinegar
- 1 teaspoon fine sea salt
- 1/2 teaspoon ground black pepper
- 1 teaspoon smoked paprika
- 1 teaspoon onion powder

- 1/2 teaspoon garlic powder
- 1/2 pound Brussels sprouts, cleaned and halved
- 1/2 teaspoon fennel seeds
- 1 teaspoon dried basil
- 1 teaspoon dried sage

Directions

1. Firstly, marinate the beef with vegetable oil, wine vinegar, salt, black pepper, paprika, onion powder, and garlic powder. Rub the marinade into the meat and let it stay at least for 3 hours.

2. Air fry at 390 degrees F for 10 minutes. Pause the machine and add the prepared Brussels sprouts; sprinkle them with fennel seeds, basil, and sage.

3. Turn the machine to 380 degrees F; press the power button and cook for 5 more minutes. Pause the machine, stir and cook for further 10 minutes.

4. Next, remove the meat from the cooking basket and cook the vegetables a few minutes more if needed and according to your taste. Serve with your favorite mayo sauce.

71. ALL-IN-ONE SPICY SPAGHETTI WITH BEEF

4 Servings

Ready in about
30 minutes

PER SERVING:
359 Calories; 5.5g Fat;
59.9g Carbs; 16.9g
Protein; 2.7g Sugars

Ground beef in a palatable spicy sauce over warm spaghetti! This staple food of Italy would win your heart!

Ingredients

- 3/4 pound ground chuck
- 1 onion, peeled and finely chopped
- 1 teaspoon garlic paste
- 1 bell pepper, chopped
- 1 small-sized habanero pepper, deveined and finely minced
- 1/2 teaspoon dried rosemary

- 1/2 teaspoon dried marjoram
- 1 ¼ cups crushed tomatoes, fresh or canned
- 1/2 teaspoon sea salt flakes
- 1/4 teaspoon ground black pepper, or more to taste
- 1 package cooked spaghetti, to serve

Directions

1. In the Air Fryer baking dish, place the ground meat, onion, garlic paste, bell pepper, habanero pepper, rosemary, and the marjoram.

2. Air-fry, uncovered, for 10 to 11 minutes. Next step, stir in the tomatoes along with salt and pepper; cook 17 to 20 minutes. Serve over cooked spaghetti. Bon appétit!

72. BEER-BRAISED SHORT LOIN

4 Servings

Ready in about
15 minutes

PER SERVING:
379 Calories; 16.4g Fat;
3.7g Carbs; 46.0g Protein;
0.0g Sugars

There are many ways to tenderize beef cuts. You can use soda, coffee, tea, tomato based sauce, buttermilk, yogurt, and so on. If you prefer an acid based marinade, use glass dishes to prevent any chemical reactions.

Ingredients

- 1 ½ pounds short loin
- 2 tablespoons olive oil
- 1 bottle beer

- 2-3 cloves garlic, finely minced
- 2 Turkish bay leaves

Directions

1. Pat the beef dry; then, tenderize the beef with a meat mallet to soften the fibers. Place it in a large-sized mixing dish.

2. Add the remaining ingredients; toss to coat well and let it marinate for at least 1 hour.

3. Cook about 7 minutes at 395 degrees F; after that, pause the Air Fryer. Flip the meat over and cook for another 8 minutes, or until it's done.

4 Servings

Ready in about
20 minutes

PER SERVING:
236 Calories; 13.7g Fat;
4.0g Carbs; 23.8g Protein;
1.0g Sugars

Too busy to cook? You can simply whip up leftovers, vegetable and eggs for lunch. For this recipe, utilize leftover beef like beef burgers, steak, pulled beef brisket, etc.

Ingredients

- Non-stick cooking spray
- 1/2 pound leftover beef, coarsely chopped
- 2 garlic cloves, pressed
- 1 cup kale, torn into pieces and wilted
- 1 tomato, chopped
- 1/4 teaspoon brown sugar

- 4 eggs, beaten
- 4 tablespoons heavy cream
- 1/2 teaspoon turmeric powder
- Salt and ground black pepper, to your liking
- 1/8 teaspoon ground allspice

Directions

1. Spritz the inside of four ramekins with a cooking spray.

2. Divide all of the above ingredients among the prepared ramekins. Stir until everything is well combined.

3. Air-fry at 360 degrees F for 16 minutes; check with a wooden stick and return the eggs to the Air Fryer for a few more minutes as needed. Serve immediately.

74. HEARTY BEEF CUBES WITH VEGETABLES

4 Servings

Ready in about
20 minutes +
marinating time

PER SERVING:
325 Calories; 17.4g Fat;
3.5g Carbs; 37.8g Protein;
1.1g Sugars

This recipe adds a whole new dimension to the art of air-frying! You can prepare a full meal using just one machine. Incredible!

Ingredients

- 1 pound top round steak, cut into cubes
- 2 tablespoons olive oil
- 1 tablespoon apple cider vinegar
- 1 teaspoon fine sea salt
- 1/2 teaspoon ground black pepper
- 1 teaspoon shallot powder
- 3/4 teaspoon smoked cayenne pepper

- 1/2 teaspoon garlic powder
- 1/4 teaspoon ground cumin
- 1/4 pound broccoli, cut into florets
- 1/4 pound mushrooms, sliced
- 1 teaspoon dried basil
- 1 teaspoon celery seeds

Directions

1. Firstly, marinate the beef with olive oil, vinegar, salt, black pepper, shallot powder, cayenne pepper, garlic powder, and cumin. Toss to coat well and let it stay for at least 3 hours.

2. Place the beef cubes in the Air Fryer cooking basket; cook at 365 degrees F for 12 minutes. Pause the machine, check the cubes for doneness and transfer them to a bowl.

3. Now, clean the cooking basket and place the vegetables in; sprinkle them with basil and celery seeds; toss to coat.

4. Set the temperature to 400 degrees F; cook for 5 to 6 minutes or until the vegetables are warmed through.

5. Serve with reserved meat cubes. Bon appétit!

75. EASY GRILLED BEEF RIBS

4 Servings

Ready in about
20 minutes +
marinating time

PER SERVING:
459 Calories; 34.4g Fat;
1.0g Carbs; 34.7g Protein;
0.0g Sugars

This could be the only recipe for beef ribs you'll ever need! Quick, easy and delicious!

Ingredients

- 1 pound meaty beef ribs
- 3 tablespoons apple cider vinegar
- 1 cup coriander, finely chopped
- 1 heaping tablespoon fresh basil leaves, chopped
- 2 garlic cloves, finely chopped

- 1 chipotle powder
- 1 teaspoon fennel seeds
- 1 teaspoon hot paprika
- Kosher salt and black pepper, to your liking
- 1/2 cup vegetable oil

Directions

1. First of all, rinse the ribs and dry them using paper towels.

2. Place all of the above ingredients in a mixing dish; toss to coat well.

3. Cover and refrigerate for at least 3 hours. Discard the marinade and place your ribs on an Air Fryer grill pan.

4. Now, set your Air Fryer to cook at 360 degrees F. Cook for 8 minutes; check for doneness and cook for another 3 to 5 minutes. Garnish with the remaining marinade and serve right away!

FISH & SEAFOOD

86

80

77

89

83

4 Servings

Ready in about
20 minutes

PER SERVING:
463 Calories; 20.3g
Fat; 46.0g Carbs; 25.0g
Protein; 2.3g Sugars

When it comes to the fried food, fish fillets are a must! The almond sauce will take these fillets over the top!

Ingredients

- 4 skin-on snapper fillets
- Sea salt and ground pepper, to taste
- 1 cup breadcrumbs
- 2 tablespoons fresh cilantro, chopped
- 1 cup all-purpose flour
- 2 medium-sized eggs

For the Almond sauce:

- 1/4 cup almonds
- 2 garlic cloves, pressed
- 1 bread slice, chopped
- 1 cup tomato paste
- 1 teaspoon dried dill weed
- 1/2 teaspoon salt
- 1/4 teaspoon freshly ground mixed peppercorns
- 1/2 cup olive oil

Directions

1. Season fish fillets with sea salt and pepper.

2. In a shallow plate, thoroughly combine the breadcrumbs and fresh chopped cilantro.

3. In another shallow plate, whisk the eggs until frothy; Place the sifted flour into a third plate.

4. Dip the fish fillets in the flour, then in the egg; afterward, coat them with breadcrumbs. Set the Air Fryer to cook at 390 degrees F; air fry for 14 to 16 minutes or until crisp.

5. To make the sauce, chop the almonds in a food processor. Add the remaining sauce ingredients, but not the olive oil.

6. Blitz for 30 seconds; then, slowly and gradually pour in the oil; process until smooth and even. Serve with the prepared snapper fillets. Bon appétit!

77. ITALIAN-STYLE COD FILLETS

4 Servings

Ready in about
15 minutes

PER SERVING:
181 Calories; 8.1g Fat;
3.0g Carbs; 23.8g Protein;
1.1g Sugars

There's nothing like fried fish fillets. This mouth-watering cod fish, coated with herby creamed sauce, is ready in about 15 minutes. Lovely!

Ingredients

- 4 cod fillets
- 1/4 teaspoon fine sea salt
- 1/4 teaspoon ground black pepper, or more to taste
- 1 teaspoon cayenne pepper
- 1/2 cup non-dairy milk

- 1/2 cup fresh Italian parsley, coarsely chopped
- 1 teaspoon dried basil
- 1/2 teaspoon dried oregano
- 1 Italian pepper, chopped
- 4 garlic cloves, minced

Directions

1. Coat the inside of a baking dish with a thin layer of vegetable oil.

2. Season the cod fillets with salt, pepper, and cayenne pepper.

3. Next, puree the remaining ingredients in your food processor. Toss the fish fillets with this mixture.

4. Set the Air Fryer to cook at 380 degrees F. Cook for 10 to 12 minutes or until the cod flakes easily. Bon appétit!

78. HONEY-GLAZED HALIBUT STEAKS

4 Servings

Ready in about
15 minutes

PER SERVING:
304 Calories; 20.7g Fat;
8.8g Carbs; 22.1g Protein;
8.7g Sugars

Halibut is a good source of omega-3 fatty acids, B vitamins,
and many others essential nutrients. It is great for your immune system
and your cardiovascular system.

Ingredients

- 1 pound halibut steaks
- Salt and pepper, to your liking
- 1 teaspoon dried basil
- 2 tablespoons honey
- 1/4 cup vegetable oil

- 2 ½ tablespoons Worcester sauce
- 1 tablespoon freshly squeezed lemon juice
- 2 tablespoons vermouth
- 1 tablespoon fresh parsley leaves, coarsely chopped

Directions

1. Place all the ingredients in a large-sized mixing dish. Gently stir to coat the fish evenly.

2. Set your Air Fryer to cook at 390 degrees F; roast for 5 minutes. Pause the machine and flip the fish over.

3. Then, cook for another 5 minutes; check for doneness and cook for a few more minutes as needed. Serve with a rich potato salad. Bon appétit!

79. CRUNCHY SALTINE FISH FILLETS

4 Servings

Ready in about
15 minutes

PER SERVING:
236 Calories; 15.7g Fat;
8.6g Carbs; 16.5g Protein;
0.0g Sugars

This recipe works with any kind of white fish like flounder, cod, haddock, etc. Use a plastic bag and a rolling pin to crush saltine crackers.

Ingredients

- 1 cup crushed saltines
- 1/4 cup extra-virgin olive oil
- 1 teaspoon garlic powder
- 1/2 teaspoon shallot powder

- 1 egg, well whisked
- 4 white fish fillets
- Salt and ground black pepper, to taste
- Fresh Italian parsley, to serve

Directions

1. Thoroughly combine the crushed saltines and olive oil in a shallow bowl.

2. In another bowl, combine the garlic powder, shallot powder, and the beaten egg.

3. Generously season the fish fillets with salt and pepper. Dip each fillet into the beaten egg.

4. Then, roll the fillets over the crumb mixture. Set your Air Fryer to cook at 370 degrees F. Air-fry for 10 to 12 minutes. Serve garnished with fresh parsley and enjoy!

80. MARINATED SARDINES WITH ROASTED POTATOES

4 Servings

Ready in about
1 hour 15 minutes

PER SERVING:
426 Calories; 27.2g
Fat; 24.5g Carbs; 21.5g
Protein; 2.1g Sugars

This is one of the family favorites, however, much healthier version! And the best part is – you can have a perfect fish with potatoes without slaving over a hot stove.

Ingredients

- 3/4 pound sardines, cleaned and rinsed
- Salt and ground black pepper, to savor
- 1 teaspoon smoked cayenne pepper
- 1 tablespoon lemon juice
- 1 tablespoon soy sauce
- 2 tablespoons olive oil

For the Potatoes:

- 8 medium Russet potatoes, peeled and quartered
- 1/2 stick melted butter
- Salt and pepper, to savor
- 1 teaspoon granulated garlic

Directions

1. Firstly, pat the sardines dry with a kitchen towel. Add salt, black pepper, cayenne pepper, lemon juice, soy sauce, and olive oil; marinate them for 30 minutes.

2. Air-fry the sardines at 350 degrees F for approximately 5 minutes. Increase the temperature to 385 degrees F and air-fry them for further 7 to 8 minutes. Then put the sardines in a nice serving platter.

3. Clean the Air Fryer cooking basket; add the potatoes, butter, salt, pepper, and garlic. Roast at 390 degrees F for 30 minutes. Serve with the prepared sardines. Bon appétit!

81. GARLICKY GRILLED SHRIMP

4 Servings

Ready in about
35 minutes

PER SERVING:
188 Calories; 8.9g Fat;
3.5g Carbs; 23.1g Protein;
0.0g Sugars

If you want to serve this amazing, briny-tasting shrimp as an appetizer, just add cocktail sticks. You can also serve it with warm angel hair pasta and create an extraordinary family lunch!

Ingredients

- 18 shrimps, shelled and deveined
- 2 tablespoons freshly squeezed lemon juice
- 1/2 teaspoon hot paprika
- 1/2 teaspoon salt
- 1 teaspoon lemon-pepper seasoning

- 2 tablespoons extra-virgin olive oil
- 2 garlic cloves, peeled and minced
- 1 teaspoon onion powder
- 1/4 teaspoon cumin powder
- 1/2 cup fresh parsley, coarsely chopped

Directions

1. Place all the ingredients in a mixing dish; gently stir, cover and let it marinate for 30 minutes in the refrigerator.

2. Air-fry in the preheated Air Fryer at 400 degrees F for 5 minutes or until the shrimps turn pink.

3. Serve over cooked pasta if desired.

82. SALMON FILLETS WITH SWEET POTATOES

4 Servings

Ready in about
45 minutes

PER SERVING:
321 Calories; 17.5g Fat;
8.2g Carbs; 34.0g Protein;
0.6g Sugars

If you are craving rich and satisfying dinner, serve salmon fillets with roasted sweet potato wedges. Classy and absolutely delicious. You can't go wrong.

Ingredients

For the Salmon Fillets:

- 4 (6-ounce) skin-on salmon fillets
- 1 tablespoon extra-virgin olive oil
- 1 teaspoon celery salt
- 1/4 teaspoon ground black pepper, or more to taste
- 2 tablespoons capers
- A pinch of dry mustard
- A pinch of ground mace
- 1 teaspoon smoked cayenne pepper

For the Potatoes:

- 4 sweet potatoes, peeled and cut into wedges
- 1 tablespoon sesame oil
- Kosher salt and pepper, to taste

Directions

1. Firstly, brush the salmon filets with the oil on all sides. Add all seasonings for the fillets.

2. Air-fry at 360 degrees F for 5 minutes; pause the Air Fryer and cook for 5 more minutes.

3. Toss the sweet potatoes with sesame oil, salt, and pepper; air-fry them at 380 degrees F for 15 minutes.

4. Now, pause the machine, flip the potatoes over and cook additional 15 to 20 minutes. Serve with salmon fillets and enjoy!

83. FANCY COCONUT CURRIED PRAWNS

4 Servings

Ready in about
10 minutes

PER SERVING:
239 Calories; 9.3g Fat;
18.6g Carbs; 19.1g
Protein; 1.4g Sugars

This is a classic! Fresh, aromatic and delicious seafood at your fingertips! It would be a perfect dish for a cocktail party, family dinner, Sunday brunch...

Ingredients

- 12 prawns, cleaned and deveined
- Salt and ground black pepper, to your liking
- 1/2 teaspoon cumin powder
- 1 teaspoon fresh lemon juice
- 1 medium-sized egg, whisked
- 1/3 cup of beer

- 1/2 cup all-purpose flour
- 1 teaspoon baking powder
- 1 tablespoon curry powder
- 1/2 teaspoon grated fresh ginger
- 1 cup flaked coconut

Directions

1. Toss the prawns with salt, pepper, cumin powder, and lemon juice.

2. In a mixing dish, place the whisked egg, beer, 1/4 cup of flour, baking powder, curry, and the ginger; mix to combine well.

3. In another mixing dish, place the remaining 1/4 cup of flour; put the flaked coconut into a third bowl.

4. Now, dip the prawns in the flour holding them by the tails. Then, dip them in the beer mix; afterwards, roll your prawns over flaked coconut.

5. Air-fry at 360 degrees F for 5 minutes; turn them over, press the power button again and cook for additional 2 to 3 minutes. Bon appétit!

84. TILAPIA FILETS WITH CREAMY CAPER SAUCE

4 Servings

Ready in about
15 minutes

PER SERVING:
215 Calories; 13.1g Fat;
3.5g Carbs; 21.5g Protein;
0.6g Sugars

This is 4-easy steps recipe that will take only 15 minutes. The sauce is so glamorous but super easy to put together!

Ingredients

- 4 tilapia fillets
- 1 tablespoon extra-virgin olive oil
- Celery salt, to taste
- Freshly cracked pink peppercorns, to taste

For the Creamy Caper Sauce:

- 1/2 cup crème fraîche
- 2 tablespoons mayonnaise
- 1/4 cup Cottage cheese, at room temperature
- 1 tablespoon capers, finely chopped

Directions

1. Toss the tilapia fillets with olive oil, celery salt, and cracked peppercorns until they are well coated.

2. Place the fillets in a single layer at the bottom of the Air Fryer cooking basket. Air-fry at 360 degrees F for about 12 minutes; turn them over once during cooking.

3. Meanwhile, prepare the sauce by mixing the remaining items.

4. Lastly, garnish air-fried tilapia fillets with the sauce and serve immediately!

4 Servings

Ready in about
15 minutes +
marinating time

PER SERVING:
174 Calories; 6.3g Fat;
7.7g Carbs; 19.8g Protein;
3.2g Sugars

For this recipe, use good sesame oil, mixed peppercorns, and fresh garlic, and you'll get a perfectly tender, flaky flounder. Serve with steamed asparagus if desired.

Ingredients

- 4 flounder fillets
- Sea salt and freshly cracked mixed peppercorns, to taste
- 1 ½ tablespoons dark sesame oil
- 2 tablespoons sake

- 1/4 cup soy sauce
- 1 tablespoon grated lemon rind
- 2 garlic cloves, minced
- 1 teaspoon brown sugar
- Fresh chopped chives, to serve

Directions

1. Place all the ingredients, without the chives, in a large-sized mixing dish. Cover and allow it to marinate for about 2 hours in your fridge.

2. Remove the fish from the marinade and cook in the Air Fryer cooking basket at 360 degrees F for 10 to 12 minutes; flip once during cooking.

3. Pour the remaining marinade into a pan that is preheated over a medium-low heat; let it simmer, stirring continuously, until it has thickened.

4. Pour the prepared glaze over flounder and serve garnished with fresh chives.

86. FISH FINGERS WITH DIJONNAISE SAUCE

4 Servings

Ready in about
15 minutes

PER SERVING:
377 Calories; 18.4g
Fat; 31.9g Carbs; 20.9g
Protein; 2.3g Sugars

This is a child-friendly recipe so invite your child in the kitchen to help you cook
these amazing fish fingers. Let's be creative!

Ingredients

For the Fish:

- 3/4 pound white fish, cut into strips
- 1 ½ tablespoons olive oil
- 1/2 teaspoon garlic salt
- 1 teaspoon red pepper flakes, crushed
- 1/2 teaspoon dried dill weed
- 1 cup all-purpose flour
- 2 medium-sized eggs, well whisked
- 3/4 cup tortilla chip crumbs

For the Dijonnaise Sauce:

- 1 ½ tablespoons Dijon mustard
- 1/2 cup mayonnaise
- 1/2 teaspoon lemon juice, freshly squeezed

Directions

1. Rub the fish strips with olive oil, salt, red pepper and dill weed. Then, prepare three shallow bowls.

2. Put the sifted flour into the first bowl. In another shallow bowl, place the eggs; in the third one, the tortilla chip crumbs.

3. Meanwhile, preheat your machine to cook at 385 degrees F. Cover the fish strips with the flour, and then with the eggs; finally, roll each fish piece over the crumbs.

4. Air-fry for 5 minutes, then pause the machine, flip them over and cook for another 5 minutes or until cooked through.

5. In the meantime, make the Dijonnaise sauce by mixing together all sauce ingredients. Serve as a dipping sauce and enjoy!

4 Servings

Ready in about
1 hour 20 minutes

PER SERVING:
210 Calories; 4.5g Fat;
25.1g Carbs; 16.2g
Protein; 3.5g Sugars

Use your blender or food processor to finely chop fish. These fish cakes are less gooey because they get their crisp crunch from the vegetables.

Ingredients

- 1 ½ cups whitefish fillets, minced
- 1 ½ cups green beans, finely chopped
- 1/2 cup scallions, chopped
- 1 chili pepper, deveined and minced
- 1 tablespoon red curry paste
- 1 teaspoon brown sugar
- 1 tablespoon fish sauce

- 2 tablespoons apple cider vinegar
- 1 teaspoon water
- Sea salt flakes, to taste
- 1/2 teaspoon cracked black peppercorns
- 1 ½ teaspoons butter, at room temperature
- Grated rind of 1 lemon
- Breadcrumbs

Directions

1. Add all ingredients in the order listed above to the mixing dish. Mix to combine well using a spatula or your hands.

2. Form into small cakes and chill for 1 hour. Place a piece of aluminum foil over the cooking basket. Place the cakes on foil.

3. Cook at 390 degrees F for 10 minutes; pause the machine, flip each fish cake over and air-fry for additional 5 minutes. Mound a cucumber relish onto the plates; add the fish cakes and serve warm.

88. TRADITIONAL FILIPINO BISTEK

4 Servings

Ready in about
10 minutes +
marinating time

PER SERVING:
242 Calories; 13.4g Fat;
9.2g Carbs; 22.7g Protein;
5.5g Sugars

You will love this recipe even if you are not much of a fish lover. It would be great if you could use calamansi juice because of its mild taste but you can't go wrong with freshly squeezed lime juice.

Ingredients

- A belly of 2 milkfish, deboned and sliced into 4 portions
- 3/4 teaspoon salt
- 1/4 teaspoon ground black pepper
- 1/4 teaspoon cumin powder
- 2 tablespoons calamansi juice
- 2 lemongrass, trimmed and cut crosswise into small pieces

- 1/2 cup tamari sauce
- 2 tablespoons fish sauce (Patis)
- 2 tablespoons brown sugar
- 1 teaspoon garlic powder
- 1/2 cup chicken broth
- 2 tablespoons olive oil

Directions

1. Firstly, pat the fish dry using kitchen towels. Put the fish into a large-sized mixing dish; add the remaining ingredients and marinate for 3 hours in the refrigerator.

2. Cook the fish steaks on an Air Fryer grill basket at 340 degrees F for 5 minutes.

3. Pause the machine, flip the steaks over and set the timer for 4 more minutes. Cook until the color turns medium brown. Serve over steamed white rice.

89. CHUNKY FISH AND CELERY CAKES

4 Servings

Ready in about
10 minutes +
chilling time

PER SERVING:
184 Calories; 7.5g Fat;
5.5g Carbs; 22.2g Protein;
0.9g Sugars

Turn a can of tuna or other fish into these delicious cakes for a quick and easy weeknight meal. They are great dipped in Dijonnaise sauce!

Ingredients

- 2 cans canned fish
- 2 celery stalks, trimmed and finely chopped
- 1 egg, whisked
- 1 cup soft bread crumbs
- 1 teaspoon whole-grain mustard

- 1/2 teaspoon sea salt
- 1/4 teaspoon freshly cracked black peppercorns
- 1 teaspoon paprika

Directions

1. Mix all of the above ingredients in the order listed above; mix to combine well and shape into four cakes; chill for 50 minutes.

2. Place on an Air Fryer grill pan. Spritz each cake with a non-stick cooking spray, covering all sides.

3. Grill at 360 degrees F for 5 minutes; then, pause the machine, flip the cakes over and set the timer for another 3 minutes. Serve over mashed potatoes.

90. JUMBO SHRIMP WITH CHIPOTLE-DIJON SAUCE

4 Servings

Ready in about
10 minutes

PER SERVING:
270 Calories; 12.2g
Fat; 10.0g Carbs; 29.1g
Protein; 2.1g Sugars

This sophisticated dish may become your weeknight favorite. A sharp-flavored chipotle-mustard sauce gives the dish a unique and irresistible flavor!

Ingredients

- 12 jumbo shrimps
- 1/2 teaspoon garlic salt
- 1/4 teaspoon freshly cracked mixed peppercorns

For the Sauce:

- 1 teaspoon Dijon mustard
- 4 tablespoons mayonnaise
- 1 teaspoon lemon rind, grated
- 1 teaspoon chipotle powder
- 1/2 teaspoon cumin powder

Directions

1. Season your shrimp with garlic salt and cracked peppercorns.

2. Now, air-fry them in the cooking basket at 395 degrees F for 5 minutes. After that, pause the machine. Flip them over and set the timer for 2 more minutes.

3. Meanwhile, mix all ingredients for the sauce; whisk to combine well. Serve with the warm shrimps. Bon appétit!

VEGAN

95

99

102

93

105

91. PERFECT VEGETABLE KEBABS

4 Servings

Ready in about
20 minutes

PER SERVING:
249 Calories; 14.2g Fat;
29.1g Carbs; 3.0g Protein;
7.1g Sugars

Colorful and delicious vegan kebabs! Make sure to soak the bamboo skewers in
water at least 2 hours before using them.

Ingredients

- 3 medium-sized carrots, cut into thick slices
- 2 parsnips, cut into thick slices
- 1 fennel, diced
- 1 teaspoon whole grain mustard
- 2 cloves garlic, pressed
- 1 red onion, cut into wedges

- 2 tablespoons dry white wine
- 1/4 cup sesame oil
- 1 teaspoon sea salt flakes
- 1/2 teaspoon ground black pepper
- 1 teaspoon smoked paprika

Directions

1. Place all of the above ingredients in a mixing dish; toss to coat well. Alternately thread vegetables onto the bamboo skewers.

2. Cook on the Air Fryer grill pan for 15 minutes at 380 degrees F. Flip them over halfway through the cooking time.

3. Taste, adjust the seasonings and serve warm.

92. CAULIFLOWER WITH SESAME AND CORN

4 Servings

Ready in about
25 minutes

PER SERVING:
131 Calories; 5.1g Fat;
20.3g Carbs; 4.3g Protein;
4.5g Sugars

To make cauliflower crumbles, you can use a cheese grater or a food processor. If you want to skip the rice, cauliflower rice is a perfect alternative. You will love it!

Ingredients

- 2 cups cauliflower crumbles
- 1 onion, peeled and finely chopped
- 1 tablespoon sesame oil
- 3 tablespoons tamari sauce
- 3 cloves garlic, peeled and pressed
- 1 tablespoon ginger, freshly grated
- 1 tablespoon fresh parsley, finely chopped
- 1/3 cup of lime juice
- 1 ½ cups frozen corn kernels
- 1 tablespoon sesame seeds

Directions

1. Combine the cauliflower crumbles, onion, sesame oil, tamari sauce, garlic, and the ginger in a mixing dish; stir until everything's well incorporated.

2. Air-fry at 400 degrees F for 12 minutes.

3. Pause the Air Fryer. Add the parsley, lemon juice, and corn. Turn the machine to cook at 390 degrees F; cook additional 10 minutes.

4. Meanwhile, toast the sesame seeds in a non-stick skillet; stir them constantly over a medium-low flame. Sprinkle over prepared cauliflower crumbles and serve warm.

93. INDIAN-STYLE FRITTERS (BHAJI)

4 Servings

Ready in about
40 minutes

PER SERVING:
214 Calories; 4.0g Fat;
36.0g Carbs; 10.3g
Protein; 7.7g Sugars

This is such a comforting dish with gram flour, onions, and Indian green chili.
Being vegan is so easy!

Ingredients

- 1 cup garbanzo bean flour (gram flour)
- 1/3 teaspoon baking powder
- 1 teaspoon curry paste
- Salt and pepper, to your liking

- 2 red onions, chopped
- 1 Indian green chili, pureed
- Non-stick cooking spray

Directions

1. Place the first 4 ingredients in a mixing dish; to make the thick batter, add cold water

2. Now, add onions and chili pepper; mix until everything is well incorporated.

3. Shape the balls and slightly press them to make the patties. Spritz the patties with cooking oil on all sides.

4. Place a sheet of aluminum foil in the Air Fryer food basket. Place the fritters on foil.

5. Then, air-fry them at 360 degrees F for 15 minutes; flip them over, press the power button and cook for another 20 minutes. Serve right away!

94. ROASTED SWEET POTATOES WITH GARLIC MAYO

 4 Servings

 Ready in about 30 minutes

PER SERVING:
303 Calories; 11.2g Fat;
49.2g Carbs; 2.6g Protein;
2.7g Sugars

This cold-weather comfort food is simply irresistible! You can serve it as a warm appetizer but, it could probably become your main dish.

Ingredients

- 8 sweet potatoes, cut into wedges
- 1 teaspoon peanut oil
- 1/2 teaspoon celery salt
- 1/4 teaspoon red pepper flakes, crushed
- 1/2 cup vegan mayonnaise
- 1 clove garlic, minced
- 1 teaspoon lemon juice

Directions

1. Toss sweet potatoes with peanut oil, celery salt, and red pepper flakes.

2. Air-fry them at 380 degrees F for 10 minutes. Shake the cooking basket and cook for 20 minutes more.

3. In the meantime, thoroughly combine the mayonnaise, garlic, and lemon juice.

4. When the sweet potato wedges come out of the Air Fryer, check them for doneness. Serve with garlic mayonnaise and enjoy!

95. YUMMY CARROT STICKS WITH HUMMUS

2 Servings

Ready in about
20 minutes

PER SERVING:
137 Calories; 6.8g Fat;
18.4g Carbs; 1.6g Protein;
9.0g Sugars

As a dinner or on-the-go combo, these carrots will satisfy your hunger during busy days. It will be ready in less than 20 minutes. Lovely!

Ingredients

- 5 carrots, washed, debris removed and sliced lengthways
- 1 teaspoon sea salt flakes
- 1/2 teaspoon white pepper

- 1/4 teaspoon dried dill weed
- 1 tablespoon sesame oil
- Humus, for dipping

Directions

1. Start by preheating your Air Fryer to cook at 370 degrees F.

2. Toss the carrots with sea salt flakes, white pepper, dill, sesame oil, covering them on all sides.

3. Now, air-fry them in the cooking basket for 12 minutes; shake the basket halfway through the cooking time.

4. Serve warm with hummus (store-bought or homemade) for dipping. Bon appétit!

96. HEARTY ASPARAGUS AND TOFU SCRAMBLE

2 Servings

Ready in about
15 minutes

PER SERVING:
160 Calories; 10.8g Fat;
8.5g Carbs; 8.9g Protein;
3.5g Sugars

If you like to experiment with scramble recipes, you should try this one. This whole dish comes together in the Air Fryer!

Ingredients

- 1 tablespoon sesame oil
- 10 ounces soft silken tofu, drained and chopped
- 6 ounces asparagus, chopped
- 2 garlic cloves, finely minced
- 1 teaspoon fresh lemon juice

- 1 tablespoon soy sauce
- 1/2 teaspoon paprika
- 1/2 teaspoon coarse salt
- Freshly cracked mixed peppercorns, to taste
- 1/2 cup fresh basil, roughly chopped

Directions

1. Grease a baking dish using the sesame oil. Now, add in the tofu and cook for 8 minutes at 370 degrees F.

2. Stir in the other ingredients, except the basil leaves; cook for a further 6 minutes.

3. Serve warm garnished with fresh basil leaves. Bon appétit!

97. MEDITERRANEAN ROASTED POTATOES

2 Servings

Ready in about
15 minutes

PER SERVING:
240 Calories; 10.9g Fat;
34.1g Carbs; 3.8g Protein;
2.4g Sugars

A hot air circulates around potatoes so they get super crispy! Enjoy these outstanding, rich, Mediterranean flavors.

Ingredients

- 4 Russet potatoes, peeled and cut into wedges
- 1 tablespoon olive oil
- 1 teaspoon fresh lemon juice
- 2 sprigs thyme, chopped
- 1 sprig rosemary, chopped

- 1 teaspoon oregano
- 1/2 teaspoon basil
- 1/2 teaspoon seasoned salt
- 1/4 teaspoon freshly cracked peppercorns
- Kalamata olives, for garnish

Directions

1. Toss the potatoes with all the remaining ingredients but not the olives.

2. Air-fry them at 360 degrees F for 10 minutes.

3. Pause the machine and shake the basket; cook for additional 3 minutes. Serve warm with Kalamata olives.

98. TOFU SCRAMBLE SPRING ROLLS

4 Servings

Ready in about
25 minutes

PER SERVING:
335 Calories; 11.5g
Fat; 41.5g Carbs; 20.4g
Protein; 4.0g Sugars

This intensely flavored food makes a great breakfast for your family. Also, you can add chili peppers to spice them up.

Ingredients

- 4 pieces spring roll rice paper wrappers
- 1 (14-ounce) package extra-firm tofu, rinsed and pressed
- 1 sweet onion, diced
- 1 cup Cremini mushrooms, cleaned and sliced
- 1/4 cup fresh parsley, minced
- Salt and black pepper, to taste

- 1/2 teaspoon turmeric powder
- 1/4 teaspoon cumin powder
- 1/2 teaspoon dried dill weed
- 1 sweet bell pepper, deveined and sliced
- 2 tablespoons nutritional yeast
- 2 tablespoons almond butter
- 2 tablespoons soy sauce
- 2 tablespoons coconut water

Directions

1. Lightly grease an Air Fryer baking dish using non-stick cooking oil. Now, put the tofu in; stir and cook for 8 minutes at 370 degrees F. Make sure to stir once or twice so the tofu doesn't stick to the bottom of the dish.

2. Then, put the sweet onions, mushrooms, parsley, salt, pepper, turmeric, cumin, dill, bell pepper, and nutritional yeasts; set the timer for 6 more minutes and press the power button.

3. In the meantime, whisk the other ingredients in a small mixing dish. Lay the rice paper wrappers flat on a work surface and fill with the prepared veggie tofu scramble.

4. Wrap the rolls and dip each one into the almond butter mixture. Air-fry at 355 degrees F for about 10 minutes; check for doneness and cook for a few minutes longer if needed. Bon appétit!

99. DELICIOUS BALLS WITH VEGAN CHEESE

6 Servings

Ready in about
30 minutes

PER SERVING:
313 Calories; 18.6g Fat;
31.9g Carbs; 4.3g Protein;
0.0g Sugars

Forget about fast food and make these homemade vegan balls! Cheap and delicious, these balls are ready in about 30 minutes.

Ingredients

- 2 cups of cake flour
- A pinch of salt
- 1/2 cup canola oil
- Water

- 1 cup vegan cheese, cubed
- 1/2 cup green coriander, minced
- 1/4 teaspoon cumin powder
- 1 teaspoon dried parsley flakes

Directions

1. Firstly, make the dough by mixing the flour, salt, and canola oil; add water and knead it into dough. Let it stay for about 20 minutes.

2. Divide the dough into equal size balls. Sprinkle cheese cubes with green coriander, cumin powder, and parsley.

3. Now, press the cheese cubes down into the center of the dough balls. Then, pinch the edges securely to form a ball. Repeat with the rest of the dough.

4. Lay the balls in the Air Fryer's cooking basket; spritz each ball with a cooking spray, coating on all sides. After that, cook for 8 to 10 minutes, shaking the basket once during the cooking time. Serve with your favorite vegan sauce for dipping. Bon appétit!

4 Servings

Ready in about
20 minutes

PER SERVING:
167 Calories; 5.6g Fat;
24.4g Carbs; 6.3g Protein;
1.8g Sugars

You don't have to buy veggie sticks, you can make your own!
These veggie sticks can be made with leftovers but, if you are able, try to use hearts
of palm! You won't regret it.

Ingredients

- 14 ounces canned hearts of palm, drained
- 1/4 cup seasoned breadcrumbs
- 1 ½ teaspoons soy sauce
- Salt and freshly ground black pepper, to taste
- 1 teaspoon cayenne pepper

For the Breading:

- 1 tablespoon olive oil
- 1 cup seasoned breadcrumbs
- 3/4 teaspoon dried dill weed

Directions

1. Firstly, pulse the hearts of palm in your food processor; transfer them to a bowl and add 1/4 cup seasoned breadcrumbs, soy sauce, salt, black pepper, and cayenne pepper. Roll the mixture into veggie fingers shape.

2. In another bowl, thoroughly combine the breading items.

3. Now, coat the veggie fingers with the breading, covering completely.

4. Air-fry for 15 minutes at 350 degrees F; turn them over once or twice during the cooking time. Eat with your favorite vegan sauce.

101. FALAFEL WITH VEGAN TZATZIKI

4 Servings

Ready in about
30 minutes

PER SERVING:
311 Calories; 12.5g
Fat; 35.9g Carbs; 16.2g
Protein; 8.0g Sugars

Falafel is an important part of Middle Eastern cuisine. It can be served with hummus, tahini sauce and salads. However, Greek Tzatziki works well too!

Ingredients

For the Falafel:

- 1 cup chickpea flour
- 1/4 teaspoon baking powder
- 1/3 cup warm water
- 1/2 teaspoon salt
- 1 tablespoon coriander leaves, finely chopped
- 2 tablespoons fresh lemon juice

For the Vegan Tzatziki:

- 12 ounces firm silken tofu
- 2 tablespoons lime juice, freshly squeezed
- 1/4 teaspoon ground black pepper, or more to taste
- 1/3 teaspoon sea salt flakes
- 1 teaspoon garlic powder
- 2 tablespoons olive oil
- 1 fresh cucumber, grated
- 1 tablespoon fresh dill, chopped

Directions

1. In a bowl, thoroughly combine all the ingredients for the falafel. Allow the mixture to stay for approximately 10 minutes.

2. Now, air-fry at 390 degrees F for 15 minutes; make sure to flip them over halfway through the cooking time.

3. To make the Vegan Tzatziki, mix silken tofu, lime juice, black pepper, and salt in your food processor. Add the garlic powder and the olive oil and mix again.

4. Stir in squeezed cucumber and dill; mix to combine well. Serve chilled with the warm falafel.

102. GOLDEN CRUNCHY TOFU CUBES

4 Servings

Ready in about
40 minutes

PER SERVING:
106 Calories; 5.4g Fat;
6.0g Carbs; 8.4g Protein;
2.0g Sugars

These tofu cubes are perfect on sandwiches, herbed rice, or all by itself. If you have the time, marinate the tofu cubes longer than 30 minutes. The longer they sit in the marinade, the more flavorful they will be!

Ingredients

- 16 ounces firm tofu, pressed and cubed
- Sea salt, to taste
- 2 tablespoons tamari sauce
- 1 tablespoon orange juice
- 3/4 teaspoon grated ginger root
- 1/2 teaspoon red chili powder
- 2 teaspoons dark toasted sesame oil
- 1 garlic clove, crushed
- 2 tablespoons tapioca starch

Directions

1. Place all the ingredients, without the tapioca starch, in a mixing bowl; let it marinate for approximately 30 minutes.

2. Next, sprinkle tapioca starch over the tofu cubes. Cook in the Air Fryer cooking basket at 375 degrees F for 10min.

3. Then, pause the machine and shake the basket to ensure that the cubes cook evenly. Bon appétit!

103. HOMEMADE POTATO CHIPS

4 Servings

Ready in about
55 minutes

PER SERVING:
157 Calories; 1.4g Fat;
33.5g Carbs; 3.6g Protein;
2.5g Sugars

There's no need to use tons of fat to make delicious crispy potato chips — an Air
Fryer is just fine. You can also experiment with spices and herbs and season them
to your liking.

Ingredients

- 4 potatoes, peeled and sliced
- 1 teaspoon canola oil

- Sea salt, to your liking

Directions

1. Soak the potatoes in cold water for 25 minutes. Place the potato slices on paper towels to pat them dry.

2. Toss them with canola oil and salt.

3. Air-fry at 390 degrees F for 20 to 25 minutes.

104. SALSA AND VEGGIE WRAPS

4 Servings

Ready in about
15 minutes

PER SERVING:
165 Calories; 5.9g Fat;
19.1g Carbs; 11.0g
Protein; 3.8g Sugars

Are you looking for more lunch options? Once you try these vegan wraps, you will make them over and over again. You can change the toppings and spices as well.

Ingredients

- 1 cup red onion, sliced
- 1 zucchini, chopped
- 1 poblano pepper, deveined and finely chopped

- 4 large-sized tortillas
- 1/2 cup salsa (homemade or store-bought)
- 4 tablespoons vegan mozzarella cheese
- Iceberg lettuce, for garnish

Directions

1. Begin by preheating your Air Fryer to 390 degrees F.

2. In a sauté pan, cook red onion, zucchini, and poblano pepper until they are tender and fragrant.

3. Divide the sautéed mixture among the 4 tortillas; spoon salsa over the top. Finish off with vegan mozzarella cheese. Wrap your tortillas around the filling.

4. Air-fry them for 7 minutes in the preheated machine, flipping over halfway through the cooking time. Serve with fresh iceberg lettuce and enjoy!

105. NUTTY AND SPICY CORN ON THE COB

4 Servings

Ready in about
15 minutes

PER SERVING:
233 Calories; 13.5g Fat;
27.0g Carbs; 7.4g Protein;
4.3g Sugars

One word: Corn! This amazing vegan dish goes either with vegan mayo or vegan mozzarella. Let your imagination run wild!

Ingredients

- 4 pieces corn on the cob, shucked
- 1 tablespoon sesame oil
- 1 tablespoon five-spice powder
- 1 teaspoon grated ginger root
- Salt and pepper, to taste
- 1 teaspoon soy sauce
- 1/2 cup walnuts, chopped and toasted

Directions

1. Brush corn with sesame oil. Now, in a small bowl, combine the five-spice powder, ginger, salt, pepper, and soy sauce.

2. Rub the corn with the spiced mixture. Arrange them on an Air Fryer grill pan and set the machine to cook at 390 degrees F.

3. Grill for 10 minutes, flipping over halfway through the cooking time. Serve garnished with chopped walnuts.

SNACKS

107

120

112

110

115

4 Servings

Ready in about
15 minutes

PER SERVING:
81 Calories; 3.9g Fat;
10.6g Carbs; 4.0g Protein;
2.5g Sugars

These Brussels sprouts are perfectly tender with a touch of mild fresh herbs and magical sesame oil. Try them as a perfect late night snack. Enjoy!

Ingredients

- 1 pound Brussels sprouts, ends and yellow leaves removed and halved lengthwise
- Salt and black pepper, to taste

- 1 tablespoon toasted sesame oil
- 1 teaspoon fennel seeds
- Chopped fresh parsley, for garnish

Directions

1. Place the Brussels sprouts, salt, pepper, sesame oil, and fennel seeds in a resealable plastic bag. Seal the bag and shake to coat.

2. Air-fry at 380 degrees F for 15 minutes or until tender. Make sure to flip them over halfway through the cooking time.

3. Serve sprinkled with fresh parsley. Bon appétit!

107. CRISPY EGGPLANT CHIPS

4 Servings

Ready in about
45 minutes

PER SERVING:
260 Calories; 14.1g Fat;
33.5g Carbs; 2.9g Protein;
9.0g Sugars

This is a great recipe for movie night at home. It is so addictive, so invite your friends over to keep yourself from eating the entire portion!

Ingredients

- 2 eggplants, peeled and thinly sliced
- Salt
- 1/2 cup tapioca starch
- 1/4 cup canola oil

- 1/2 cup water
- 1 teaspoon garlic powder
- 1/2 teaspoon dried dill weed
- 1/2 teaspoon ground black pepper, to taste

Directions

1. Salt the eggplant slices and let them stay for about 30 minutes. Squeeze the eggplant slices and rinse them under cold running water.

2. Toss the eggplant slices with the other ingredients. Cook at 390 degrees F for 13 minutes, working in batches.

3. Serve with a sauce for dipping. Bon appétit!

108. CRISPY FRIED LEEK RINGS

4 Servings

Ready in about
15 minutes

PER SERVING:
287 Calories; 7.8g Fat;
46.1g Carbs; 8.9g Protein;
5.9g Sugars

There's nothing better than crispy fried vegetables. But what about all the fat that actually goes with them? Simply make them in your Air Fryer and you'll get the same results with far fewer calories!

Ingredients

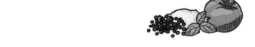

- 1 large-sized leek, cut into 1/2-inch wide rings
- Salt and pepper, to taste
- 1/2 teaspoon mustard powder
- 1 cup milk

- 1 egg
- 1 cup self-rising flour
- 3/4 teaspoon baking powder
- 1 cup crushed saltines
- 1 tablespoon olive oil

Directions

1. Toss your leeks with salt, pepper, and mustard powder. Grab three mixing bowls to set up a breading station.

2. In a mixing bowl, whisk the milk and egg until frothy and pale. Now, combine the flour and baking powder in another mixing bowl. In the third bowl, combine the crushed saltines with olive oil.

3. Coat the leek slices with the flour mixture. Dredge the floured leek slices into the milk/egg mixture, coating well. Finally, roll them over the crumb mixture.

4. Air-fry for approximately 10 minutes at 370 degrees F. Bon appétit!

109. CHEESY BROCCOLI BALLS

6 Servings

Ready in about
20 minutes

PER SERVING:
328 Calories; 14.8g
Fat; 32.2g Carbs; 16.3g
Protein; 2.1g Sugars

There is no wrong way to eat these veggie balls. You can serve them with cocktail sticks and a dipping sauce for full enjoyment!

Ingredients

- 2 eggs, well whisked
- 2 cups Colby cheese, shredded
- 1 cup all-purpose flour
- Seasoned salt, to taste

- 1/4 teaspoon ground black pepper, or more to taste
- 1 head broccoli, chopped into florets
- 1 cup crushed saltines

Directions

1. Thoroughly combine the eggs, cheese, flour, salt, pepper, and broccoli to make the consistency of dough.

2. Chill for 1 hour and shape into small balls; roll the patties over the crushed saltines. Spritz them with cooking oil on all sides.

3. Cook at 360 degrees F for 10 minutes. Check for doneness and return to the Air Fryer for 8 to 10 more minutes. Serve with a sauce for dipping. Bon appétit!

110. WINGS IN SPICY MOLASSES BARBECUE SAUCE

6 Servings

Ready in about
20 minutes

PER SERVING:
275 Calories; 10.9g Fat;
9.7g Carbs; 33.1g Protein;
7.9g Sugars

If you are looking for the recipe for Super Bowl Sunday, these spicy, sweet and sticky wings are a great idea! They get their heat from habanero hot sauce, which is simply delicious.

Ingredients

For the Sauce:

- 1 tablespoon yellow mustard
- 1 tablespoon apple cider vinegar
- 1 tablespoon olive oil
- 1/4 cup unsulfured blackstrap molasses
- 1/4 cup ketchup
- 2 tablespoons brown sugar
- 1 garlic clove, minced
- Salt and ground black pepper, to your liking
- 1/8 teaspoon ground allspice
- 1/4 cup water

For the Wings:

- 2 pounds chicken wings
- 1/4 teaspoon celery salt
- 1/4 cup habanero hot sauce
- Chopped fresh parsley, or garnish

Directions

1. In a sauté pan that is preheated over a medium-high flame, place all the ingredients for the sauce and bring it to a boil. Then, reduce the temperature and simmer until it has thickened.

2. Meanwhile, preheat your Air Fryer to 400 degrees F; cook the chicken wings for 6 minutes; flip them over and cook for additional 6 minutes. Season them with celery salt.

3. Serve with the prepared sauce and habanero hot sauce, garnished with fresh parsley leaves. Bon appétit!

111. GAME DAY SHRIMP BITES

10 Servings

Ready in about
45 minutes

PER SERVING:
376 Calories; 24.8g Fat;
2.1g Carbs; 34.0g Protein;
0.0g Sugars

This is an ultimate finger food and glorious game day snack! It pairs perfectly with a creamy homemade dipping sauce.

Ingredients

- 1 ¼ pounds shrimp, peeled and deveined
- 1 teaspoon paprika
- 1/2 teaspoon ground black pepper
- 1/2 teaspoon red pepper flakes, crushed
- 1 tablespoon salt

- 1 teaspoon chili powder
- 1 tablespoon shallot powder
- 1/4 teaspoon cumin powder
- 1 ¼ pounds thin bacon slices

Directions

1. Toss the shrimps with all the seasoning until they are coated well.

2. Next, wrap a slice of bacon around the shrimps, securing with a toothpick; repeat with the remaining ingredients; chill for 30 minutes.

3. Air-fry them at 360 degrees F for 7 to 8 minutes, working in batches. Serve with cocktail sticks if desired. Enjoy!

112. BUTTERY SAGE FINGERLING POTATOES

8 Servings

Ready in about
45 minutes

PER SERVING:
178 Calories; 6.3g Fat;
28.6g Carbs; 3.5g Protein;
1.8g Sugars

These flavorful small potatoes are a guaranteed crowd pleaser. Sage protects your immune system, alleviates skin conditions and enhances your brain health.

Ingredients

- 1 ½ pounds fingerling potatoes, halved lengthwise
- 2 tablespoons melted butter
- 1/4 cup fresh sage leaves, finely chopped
- 2 sprigs thyme, chopped

- 1 teaspoon lemon zest, finely grated
- 1/4 teaspoon ground pepper
- 1 tablespoon sea salt flakes
- 1/2 teaspoon grated ginger

Directions

1. Soak the potatoes in cold water for about 30 minutes. Then, pat them dry using a kitchen towel.

2. After that, roast at 400 degrees F for 15 minutes. Serve in a nice serving bowl, accompanied by tomato ketchup and mayonnaise. Bon appétit!

113. PECORINO BROCCOLI MELTS

6 Servings

Ready in about
20 minutes

PER SERVING:
86 Calories; 4.2g Fat;
7.3g Carbs; 7.0g Protein;
1.8g Sugars

If you are looking for healthy snack recipe, these broccoli bites are the answer! This recipe calls for Shoyu sauce – Japanese-style soy sauce that is made with soybeans and wheat. This sauce has less intensive flavor than Chinese soy sauce.

Ingredients

- 1 large-sized head of broccoli, broken into small florets
- 1/2 teaspoon sea salt
- 1/4 teaspoon ground black pepper, or more to taste
- 1 tablespoon Shoyu sauce
- 1 teaspoon groundnut oil
- 2 tablespoons Pecorino Toscano, freshly grated
- Paprika, to taste

Directions

1. Add the broccoli florets to boiling water; boil approximately 4 minutes; drain well.

2. Season with salt and pepper; drizzle with Shoyu sauce and groundnut oil.

3. Air-fry at 390 degrees F for 10 minutes; shake the Air Fryer basket, push the power button again, and continue to cook for 5 minutes more.

4. Toss the fried broccoli with the cheese and paprika. Bon appétit!

4 Servings

Ready in about
15 minutes

PER SERVING:
114 Calories; 0.6g Fat;
29.4g Carbs; 1.6g Protein;
15.1g Sugars

Before you start making this great guilt-free snack, don't forget to drizzle your bananas with fresh lemon juice. Otherwise, they will get brown quickly; further, you should add lemon juice for an extra hit of tangy, distinctive flavor. Win-Win!

Ingredients

- 4 medium-sized bananas, peeled and cut into 1/4-inch slices
- Non-stick cooking spray

- 1/2 cup freshly squeezed lemon juice
- 1/2 teaspoon ground cinnamon
- A pinch of kosher salt

Directions

1. Lightly coat the bananas with olive oil; drizzle with the freshly squeezed lemon juice.

2. Air-fry at 185 degrees F for 10 to 12 minutes.

3. Take the banana slices out of the Air Fryer; sprinkle with cinnamon and salt. Place in an airtight container for storage.

115. AROMATIC ROASTED SQUASH BITES

6 Servings

Ready in about
20 minutes

PER SERVING:
110 Calories; 4.7g Fat;
18.5g Carbs; 1.0g Protein;
6.1g Sugars

Toss the winter squash with sugar and spices for an extraordinarily tasty appetizer!
You will get all in one bite – zesty, sweet, and aromatic food!

Ingredients

- 1 ½ pounds winter squash, peeled and cut into 1/2-inch chunks
- 1/4 cup dark brown sugar
- 2 tablespoons melted coconut oil
- A pinch of coarse salt

- A pinch of pepper
- 2 tablespoons sage, finely chopped
- Zest of 1 small-sized lemon
- 1/8 teaspoon ground allspice

Directions

1. Toss the squash chunks with the other items.

2. Roast in the Air Fryer's cooking basket at 350 degrees F for 10 minutes.

3. Pause the machine, and turn the temperature to 400 degrees F; stir and roast for additional 8 minutes. Bon appétit!

116. LAST MINUTE BRUSSELS SPROUT APPETIZER

4 Servings

Ready in about
20 minutes

PER SERVING:
110 Calories; 7.4g Fat;
10.6g Carbs; 3.9g Protein;
2.5g Sugars

Prepare the healthiest chips ever and eat smart by using a rapid air technology! You can sprinkle Brussels sprout chips with lightly toasted sesame seeds if desired.

Ingredients

- 1 pound Brussels sprouts, trimmed and cut off the ends
- 1 teaspoon kosher salt

- 1 tablespoon lemon zest
- Non-stick cooking spray

Directions

1. Firstly, peel the Brussels sprouts using a small paring knife. Toss the leaves with salt and lemon zest; spritz them with a cooking spray, coating all sides.

2. Bake at 380 degrees for 8 minutes; shake the cooking basket halfway through the cooking time and cook for 7 more minutes.

3. Make sure to work in batches so everything can cook evenly. Taste and adjust the seasonings. Bon appétit!

6 Servings

Ready in about
20 minutes

PER SERVING:
294 Calories; 8.6g Fat;
26.6g Carbs; 27.0g
Protein; 7.1g Sugars

There are many exciting ways to cook meatballs. Air frying is a quick, easy, and healthy way to make these party favorites!

Ingredients

- 1/2 pound ground pork
- 1/2 pound ground beef
- 1 cup quinoa, cooked
- 1 beaten egg
- 2 scallions, finely chopped
- 1/2 teaspoon onion powder
- 1 ½ tablespoons Dijon mustard

- 3/4 cup ketchup
- 1 teaspoon ancho chili powder
- 1 tablespoon sesame oil
- 2 tablespoons tamari sauce
- 1/4 cup balsamic vinegar
- 2 tablespoons sugar

Directions

1. Mix all the ingredients until everything is well incorporated.

2. Roll into small meatballs.

3. Cook at 370 degrees F for 10 minutes. Now, shake the basket and cook for 5 minutes more.

118. CHEESY MASHED POTATO BALLS

6 Servings

Ready in about
15 minutes

PER SERVING:
371 Calories; 24.4g
Fat; 21.1g Carbs; 17.3g
Protein; 0.6g Sugars

These appetizing balls are the perfect way to give new life to your leftovers. In this recipe, you can use Italian seasoning blend as well as a few tablespoons of ground pine nuts.

Ingredients

- 3 cups mashed potatoes
- 1 egg, slightly beaten
- 2 green onions, sliced
- 1/2 cup ham, finely chopped

- 1/2 cup Colby cheese, shredded
- 8 ounces soft cheese
- 1 cup seasoned breadcrumbs
- 2 ½ tablespoons canola oil

Directions

1. Combine all the ingredients, except the breadcrumbs and canola oil, in a mixing dish. Roll the mixture into bite-sized balls.

2. Thoroughly combine the breadcrumbs with canola oil. Roll the balls over the breadcrumb mix.

3. Air-fry them at 390 degrees F for 5 minutes. Work in batches. Serve with toothpicks.

119. HARISSA AND BASIL CORN

4 Servings

Ready in about
15 minutes

PER SERVING:
168 Calories; 5.2g Fat;
29.8g Carbs; 5.3g Protein;
5.7g Sugars

Corn on the cob is popular to eat as a fast snack or a brunch. This is a basic recipe. You can use your favorite mellow cheese, fragrant fresh herbs or a homemade dipping sauce.

Ingredients

- 4 ears corn, husked and cleaned
- 2 tablespoons harissa sauce
- 1 tablespoon melted ghee

- 1 teaspoon smoked cayenne pepper
- Juice of 2 small-sized lemons
- 1 tablespoon fresh basil leaves, coarsely chopped

Directions

1. Rub the corn with harissa sauce and melted ghee. Sprinkle with cayenne pepper. Arrange them on an Air Fryer grill pan.

2. Air-fry them at 390 degrees F for 10 minutes. Pause the Air Fryer, turn the cobs over, and cook for additional 5 minutes.

3. Drizzle warm corn with fresh lemon juice and garnish with fresh basil leaves.

4. Bon appétit!

120. COCKTAIL SAUSAGE WITH SPICY MAYO SAUCE

4 Servings

Ready in about
15 minutes

PER SERVING:
304 Calories; 26.2g Fat;
4.5g Carbs; 12.4g Protein;
1.0g Sugars

It would be good if you could find high-quality pork sausages for this recipe. The tangy mayo dipping sauce gives them a special flavor twist!

Ingredients

- 1/2 pound pork cocktail sausages

For the Sauce:
- 1/4 cup mayonnaise
- 1/4 cup cream cheese
- 1 whole grain mustard
- 1 teaspoon balsamic vinegar
- 1 garlic clove, finely minced
- 1 teaspoon chili powder

Directions

1. Take your sausages, give them a few pricks using a fork and place them on the Air Fryer grill pan.

2. Set the timer for 15 minutes; after 8 minutes, pause the Air Fryer, turn the sausages over and cook for further 7 minutes.

3. Check for doneness and take the sausages out of the machine.

4. In the meantime, thoroughly combine all the ingredients for the sauce. Serve with warm sausages and enjoy!

BEANS AND GRAINS

128

130

121

134

124

4 Servings

Ready in about
10 minutes

PER SERVING:
76 Calories; 6.1g Fat; 4.8g
Carbs; 0.8g Protein; 0.0g
Sugars

If you are a huge fan of the croutons, the good news is that you can make them in your Air Fryer. They are very versatile. This recipe calls for fresh garlic but you can freely experiment with fragrant herbs, organic oils, cheese, etc.

Ingredients

- 4 slices whole-wheat stale bread, edges trimmed and cut into 1/2-inch cubes
- 1 clove garlic, finely minced

- 2 tablespoons softened butter
- 1 sprig rosemary, chopped

Directions

1. Toss the bread cubes with garlic, butter, and rosemary.

2. Cook for 3 minutes at 285 degrees F. Shake the basket and cook for a further 3 minutes.

3. Serve over favorite soups. Bon appétit!

6 Servings

Ready in about
10 minutes

PER SERVING:
191 Calories; 6.7g Fat;
27.0g Carbs; 6.7g Protein;
9.6g Sugars

If you're ready for the best breakfast prepared in an Air Fryer, try this recipe. You can substitute dried apples, pears, nectarines, or peaches for the apricot.

Ingredients

- 6 slices of French bread
- 2 tablespoons butter, at room temperature
- 1/3 cup milk
- 3 eggs, whisked

- A pinch of ground allspice
- A pinch of kosher salt
- 1/4 cup dried apricots, chopped
- Confectioners' sugar, for garnish

Directions

1. Start by preheating your Air Fryer to 380 degrees F.

2. Coat the bread slices with butter on both sides. In a mixing bowl, whisk the milk, eggs, allspice, and salt.

3. After that, soak buttered bread slices in the milk mixture for about 10 minutes. Transfer the bread slices to an Air Fryer baking dish.

4. Scatter chopped apricots over the top of each slice of bread. Spritz with a non-stick cooking spray.

5. Air-fry them for 2 minutes. Now, flip each bread slice over, spritz with the cooking spray, and cook for additional 3 minutes.

6. Afterward, dust with confectioners' sugar and serve. Bon appétit!

123. CORN AND SCALLION CAKES

6 Servings

Ready in about
15 minutes

PER SERVING:
168 Calories; 4.6g Fat;
27.4g Carbs; 5.2g Protein;
2.0g Sugars

If you've never had corn fritters from an Air Fryer, you're missing the best and the most delicious fritters ever! You can substitute spring onions for the scallions.

Ingredients

- 1 ¼ cups all-purpose flour
- 1/2 teaspoon baking soda
- 1 teaspoon baking powder
- 1/4 teaspoon sugar
- A pinch of kosher salt
- A pinch of freshly grated nutmeg
- 1 teaspoon paprika

- 1/4 teaspoon white vinegar
- 1/2 cup milk
- 1 ½ tablespoons melted butter
- 1 whole egg
- 1 ¼ cups corn kernels
- 1/4 cup cilantro, chopped
- 1/4 cup scallions, chopped

Directions

1. In a mixing bowl, combine the flour, baking soda, baking powder, sugar, salt, nutmeg, and paprika.

2. In another bowl, combine the vinegar along with the milk, butter and egg. Add this mixture to the dry mixture.

3. Preheat the Air Fryer to 380 degrees F. Stir in the corn kernels, cilantro, and the scallions. Then, shape the batter into the rounded fritters. Chill them in your freezer for 6 to 7 minutes.

4. Air-fry them for about 5 minutes and serve warm with mayonnaise.

124. PUMPKIN AND PECAN BREAKFAST MUFFINS

4 Servings

Ready in about
20 minutes

PER SERVING:
247 Calories; 16.8g Fat;
24.1g Carbs; 2.2g Protein;
13.3g Sugars

This is a whole-grain breakfast in less than 20 minutes! It's one of the perks of owning an Air Fryer! Also, you can substitute banana for pumpkin puree.

Ingredients

- 4 tablespoons cake flour
- 1/3 teaspoon baking powder
- 1/4 cup oats
- A pinch of salt
- 1/4 cup ghee, at room temperature
- 1/4 cup caster sugar

- 2 tablespoons pecans, ground
- 1/4 cup pumpkin puree
- 1/2 teaspoon freshly grated nutmeg
- 1/4 teaspoon crystalized ginger
- 1/4 teaspoon ground cinnamon

Directions

1. Mix the first 4 ingredients in a bowl.

2. In another bowl, beat the ghee with sugar; fold in the pecans and pumpkin puree, and stir again. Add this mixture to the dry flour mixture. Add the nutmeg, ginger and cinnamon, and mix again using a wide spatula.

3. You can add a little water to make a batter. Then, prepare the muffin moulds by adding muffin liners to each of them.

4. Bake the muffins at 320 degrees F for 10 minutes. Let them stay for 10 to 12 minutes before removing from the moulds. Bon appétit!

125. MEDITERRANEAN POLENTA ROUNDS

6 Servings

Ready in about
2 hours 6 minutes

PER SERVING:
203 Calories; 2.4g Fat;
40.8g Carbs; 3.9g Protein;
0.6g Sugars

Let your imagination run wild and serve these polenta rounds as colorful canapes for your next cocktail party! You can add bocconcini, shaved cheese, mushrooms, olives, and so on.

Ingredients

- 1 tablespoon butter
- 2 cups polenta, pre-cooked
- Salt and pepper, to your liking
- 1 sprig thyme, chopped
- 2 sprigs rosemary, chopped
- 1 teaspoon cayenne pepper
- 1/2 teaspoon dried basil
- 1/2 teaspoon dried oregano
- Thin slices of prosciutto, to serve
- Tomato ketchup, to serve

Directions

1. Begin by preheating your Air Fryer to 360 degrees F. Then, butter the baking dish and set aside.

2. Combine the polenta with all seasonings; scrape the mixture into the buttered baking dish and place in the refrigerator for 2 hours or until set.

3. Then, cut equal discs from the polenta using a round pastry cutter. Air-fry approximately 6 minutes.

4. Lastly, top each round with the slice of prosciutto and serve with the ketchup on the side. Bon appétit!

126. NANA'S ROSEMARY CORNBREAD

6 Servings

Ready in about
1 hour

PER SERVING:
240 Calories; 8.0g Fat;
36.2g Carbs; 6.4g Protein;
5.0g Sugars

This cornbread turns out great every time. Spice it up and add smoky chipotles or other fiery peppers to this great recipe!

Ingredients

- 1 cup cornmeal
- 1 ½ cups of flour
- 1/2 teaspoon baking soda
- 1/2 teaspoon baking powder
- 1/4 teaspoon kosher salt
- 1 teaspoon dried rosemary

- 1/4 teaspoon garlic powder
- 2 tablespoons caster sugar
- 2 eggs
- 1/4 cup melted butter
- 1 cup buttermilk
- 1/2 cup corn kernels

Directions

1. In a bowl, mix all dry ingredients until well combined. In another bowl, combine all liquid ingredients.

2. Add the liquid mix to the dry mix. Fold in the corn kernels and stir to combine well.

3. Press the batter into the round loaf pan that is lightly greased with a non-stick cooking spray.

4. Air-fry for 1 hour at 380 degrees F. Bon appétit!

127. SPICED CRUMBED BEANS

4 Servings

Ready in about
10 minutes

PER SERVING:
135 Calories; 3.1g Fat;
21.3g Carbs; 6.2g Protein;
1.2g Sugars

Here's the perfect appetizer: hot, crispy beans with big flavors! This recipe calls for a cooking spray but a little melted ghee would be welcome too.

Ingredients

- 1/2 cup all-purpose flour
- 1 teaspoon smoky chipotle powder
- 1/2 teaspoon ground black pepper
- 1 teaspoon sea salt flakes

- 2 eggs, beaten
- 1/2 cup crushed saltines
- 10 ounces wax beans

Directions

1. Mix the flour, chipotle powder, black pepper, and salt. Place the eggs in a second shallow bowl.

2. Add the crushed saltines to a third bowl. Rinse the beans under running water and remove any tough strings.

3. Dredge the beans into the flour mixture; then, coat with the beaten egg; finally, roll them over the crushed saltines.

4. Spritz the beans with a non-stick cooking spray. Air-fry at 360 degrees F for 4 minutes. Shake the cooking basket and continue to cook for 3 minutes.

128. INDIAN-STYLE ROLL-UPS

2 Servings

Ready in about
15 minutes

PER SERVING:
251 Calories; 3.6g Fat;
49.5g Carbs; 6.3g Protein;
4.2g Sugars

Who said you can't make bread rolls in an Air Fryer? Try these tender and delicious roll-ups chock full of aromatic Indian flavors. You will be delighted!

Ingredients

- 1 teaspoon vegetable oil
- 1/2 cup scallions, finely chopped
- 1/2 teaspoon curry powder
- 1/2 teaspoon cumin powder
- 2 large-sized russet potatoes, cooked and mashed

- 1/2 teaspoon mango powder
- Salt and black pepper, to your liking
- 1/2 teaspoon chaat masala
- 1/3 teaspoon lal mirchs powder
- 6 slices multi-grain bread, cut the crusts off

Directions

1. Heat the oil in a non-stick skillet over a moderate flame. Then, sauté the scallions until tender; add curry powder and cumin powder and cook for 30 seconds more, stirring constantly.

2. Remove the skillet from the heat. Add mashed potatoes to the skillet and stir to combine well. Now, stir in the remaining ingredients, except the bread slices.

3. Next, roll each slice of bread flat using a rolling pin. Divide the potato mixture among the bread slices and roll them up tightly. Secure with toothpicks. Spritz each roll with a cooking spray, coating on all sides.

4. Place seam side down on the bottom of a cooking basket.

5. Air-fry for 8 minutes at 390 degrees F. Pause the machine, flip them over and set the timer for additional 5 minutes. Eat warm with a sauce for dipping.

129. SAVORY BURRATA AND HAM MUFFINS

6 Servings

Ready in about
15 minutes

PER SERVING:
304 Calories; 2.2g Fat;
59.0g Carbs; 10.6g
Protein; 2.4g Sugars

Burrata is a semi-soft Italian cheese that is very creamy, which makes it a perfect ingredient for these chewy muffins. Beyond brunch, you might want to consider this as an appetizer for your dinner party.

Ingredients

- 1 box muffin mix
- 1/2 cup fully cooked ham, chopped
- 1/4 cup spring onions, finely chopped
- 1 teaspoon garlic powder
- 1/2 teaspoon mustard powder
- 1/2 burrata ball

Directions

1. Prepare the muffin mix as directed. Add the remaining ingredients and mix well.

2. Lightly oil a mini muffin pan using cooking spray and divide out the mixture.

3. Now, bake at 340 degrees F for about 10 minutes; pause the machine.

4. After that, check for doneness and cook for 5 more minutes or until the muffins have risen; taste with a skewer. Bon appétit!

130. HAM AND CHEESE TOAST

4 Servings

Ready in about
10 minutes

PER SERVING:
293 Calories; 24.9g Fat;
4.7g Carbs; 12.9g Protein;
0.6g Sugars

Every time you want warm and quick breakfast, you can make this toast that melts in your mouth. Add a pinch of nutmeg for a touch of sophistication!

Ingredients

- 4 slices of white sandwich bread
- 1/2 stick butter, at room temperature
- 1 teaspoon whole-grain mustard

- 8 ounces baked ham, thinly sliced
- 1 ½ cups Gruyere cheese, grated
- A pinch of nutmeg

Directions

1. Toast the bread slices; now, spread with butter and mustard.

2. Add ham and top with Gruyere cheese; afterward, add a few sprinkles of freshly grated nutmeg.

3. Air-fry them at 390 degrees F for 4 to 6 minutes. Serve warm with some extra mustard. Bon appétit!

131. CRISPY PEPPERY VEGETABLE FRITTERS

4 Servings

Ready in about
15 minutes

PER SERVING:
168 Calories; 8.5g Fat;
14.7g Carbs; 8.8g Protein;
1.8g Sugars

If you don't have all day to make dinner, the fritters are a quick and effective solution! These fritters are child-friendly but if you want to spice them up, you can add chili powder or a few dashes of Tabasco sauce.

Ingredients

- 1 cup bell peppers, deveined and chopped
- 1 teaspoon sea salt flakes
- 1 teaspoon cumin
- 1/4 teaspoon paprika
- 1/2 cup shallots, chopped
- 2 cloves garlic, minced

- 1 ½ tablespoons fresh chopped cilantro
- 1 egg, whisked
- 3/4 cup Cheddar cheese, grated
- 1/4 cup cooked quinoa
- 1/4 cup self-rising flour

Directions

1. Mix all the ingredients until everything is well incorporated. Shape into balls; then, slightly flatten each ball.

2. Spritz the patties with a cooking spray. Place the patties in a single layer in your Air Fryer cooking basket.

3. Cook at 340 degrees for 5 minutes; flip them over and cook another 5 minutes.

4. Bon appétit!

4 Servings

Ready in about
15 minutes

PER SERVING:
321 Calories; 6.9g Fat;
54.7g Carbs; 8.9g Protein;
2.0g Sugars

These protein-packed vegetarian balls are sure to please. In this recipe, try to use the mushrooms with a creamy texture and mild flavor like Oyster or Button mushrooms.

Ingredients

- 1 tablespoon rice bran oil
- 1 small-sized onion, finely chopped
- 2 garlic cloves, peeled and minced
- 1/2 cup mushrooms, finely chopped
- 6 ounces cooked rice
- Sea salt, to savor

- 1/4 teaspoon ground black pepper, or more to taste
- 1/2 teaspoon dried dill weed
- 1 teaspoon paprika
- 1 tablespoon Colby cheese, grated
- 1 egg, beaten
- 1 cup breadcrumbs

Directions

1. Warm the rice bran oil in a saucepan that is preheated over a moderate heat; sauté the onion and garlic until tender and fragrant.

2. Add in the mushrooms and cook until the liquid has almost evaporated. Allow the sautéed mixture to cool slightly; fold in the cooked rice. Add the salt, black pepper, dill, and paprika.

3. Fold in the cheese and mix again. Shape the mushroom/risotto mixture into bite-sized balls; gently flatten them with your hands. Dip them in the beaten egg; then, roll them over the breadcrumbs.

4. Air-fry the risotto balls for 7 minutes at 390 degrees F. Check for doneness and cook for 2 to 3 more minutes as needed. Serve with marinara sauce. Bon appétit!

133. AROMATIC SHRIMP AND JASMINE RISOTTO

4 Servings

Ready in about
15 minutes

PER SERVING:
232 Calories; 7.5g Fat;
31.5g Carbs; 8.9g Protein;
1.2g Sugars

Jasmine rice is a kind of fragrant rice named after the jasmine flower; it comes in two varieties – white and brown. You will love this risotto that reheats well too.

Ingredients

- 1 cup shrimps, deveined
- 1/2 cup green onion, finely chopped
- 2 cloves garlic, minced
- 1 celery stalk, trimmed and chopped
- 2 tablespoons peanut oil
- 1 tablespoon soy sauce
- 1 tablespoon oyster sauce
- 1 teaspoon brown sugar

- 1/2 teaspoon sea salt flakes
- 1/2 teaspoon red pepper flakes, crushed
- 5 ounces jasmine rice, pre-cooked
- 1 tablespoon fresh sage, chopped
- 1 tablespoon fresh thyme, chopped
- 1 tablespoon fresh basil, chopped
- 2 tablespoons fresh parsley, chopped

Directions

1. Thoroughly combine the first ten ingredients; transfer the mixture to an Air Fryer baking dish. Air-fry for 7 minutes at 390 degrees F, cooking in batches as needed.

2. Fold in the cooked rice; add the herbs and air-fry for further 7 minutes. Serve warm with sour cream. Bon appétit!

134. GOLDEN POLENTA BITES WITH FRIED VEGGIES

6 Servings	Ready in about 50 minutes	**PER SERVING:** 313 Calories; 3.5 Fat; 62.7g Carbs; 7.6g Protein; 2.6g Sugars

Slices of crispy polenta are topped with roasted vegetable and Cheddar cheese – all-in-one vegetarian bites for a summer party.

Ingredients

- 1 cup onions, chopped
- 2 cloves garlic, finely minced
- 1/2 pound zucchini, cut into bite-sized chunks
- 1/2 pound potatoes, peeled and cut into bite-sized chunks
- 1 tablespoon olive oil
- 1 teaspoon paprika

- 1/2 teaspoon salt
- 1/2 teaspoon freshly ground black pepper, or more to taste
- 1/2 teaspoon dried dill weed, or more to taste
- 14 ounces pre-cooked polenta tube, cut into slices
- 1/4 cup Cheddar cheese, shaved

Directions

1. Add the vegetables to an Air Fryer cooking basket. Sprinkle them with olive oil, paprika, salt, pepper, and dill.

2. Now, set the machine to cook at 400 degrees F. Cook for 6 minutes.

3. After that, pause the machine, shake the basket and set the timer for 6 minutes more. Set aside.

4. Next, spritz the polenta slices with non-stick cooking oil. Spritz the cooking basket too. Set your Air Fryer to cook at 400 degrees F

5. Air-fry for 20 to 25 minutes. Turn the polenta slices over and cook for another 10 minutes. Top each polenta slice with air-fried vegetables and shaved cheese. Enjoy!

135. HONEY BUTTERY DINNER ROLLS

6 Servings

Ready in about
3 hours 15 minutes

PER SERVING:
219 Calories; 9.0g Fat;
31.0g Carbs; 4.1g Protein;
9.5g Sugars

There's nothing like the warm, fluffy and moist bread rolls for family dinner. These buttery rolls will make your kitchen smell magnificent!

Ingredients

For the Rolls:

- 1 1/3 cups plain flour
- 1 ½ tablespoons white sugar
- 1 teaspoon of instant yeast
- A pinch of kosher salt
- 2 tablespoons melted butter
- 1 egg yolk
- 1/3 cup milk
- A pinch of nutmeg

For the Topping:

- 2 tablespoons softened butter
- 2 tablespoons honey

Directions

1. Mix the flour, sugar, instant yeast, and salt using a stand mixer. Whisk on low speed for 1 minute or until smooth.

2. Now, stir in the butter. Continue to mix for 1 more minute as it all combines.

3. Lay the dough onto a lightly floured surface and knead several times. Transfer the dough to a large bowl, cover and place it in a warm room to rise until doubled in size.

4. Now, whisk the egg yolk with milk and nutmeg. Coat the balls with the egg mixture.

5. Shape into balls, loosely cover and allow the balls to rise until doubled; it takes about 1 hour.

6. Then, bake them in the preheated Air Fryer at 320 degrees F for 14 to 15 minutes. In the meantime, make the topping by simply mixing the very soft butter with honey. Afterward, spread the topping onto each warm roll.

7. Cover the leftovers and keep in your fridge. Bon appétit!

DESSERTS

138

141

149

144

136

136. MINI STRAWBERRY PIES WITH SUGAR CRUST

8 Servings

Ready in about
15 minutes

PER SERVING:
237 Calories; 12.8g Fat;
28.2g Carbs; 2.7g Protein;
8.9g Sugars

There are many ways to use canned biscuit dough in an Air Fryer! You can make these delectable fresh pies for your family in 15 minutes. Incredible!

Ingredients

- 1/2 cup powdered sugar
- 1/4 teaspoon ground cloves
- 1/8 teaspoon cinnamon powder
- 1 teaspoon vanilla extract

- 1 (12-ounce) can biscuit dough
- 12 ounces strawberry pie filling
- 1/4 cup butter, melted

Directions

1. Thoroughly combine the sugar, cloves, cinnamon, and vanilla.

2. Then, stretch and flatten each piece of the biscuit dough into a round circle using a rolling pin.

3. Divide the strawberry pie filling among the biscuits. Roll up tightly and dip each biscuit piece into the melted butter; cover them with the spiced sugar mixture.

4. Brush with a non-stick cooking oil on all sides. Air-bake them at 340 degrees F for approximately 10 minutes or until they're golden brown. Let them cool for 5 minutes before serving.

137. FUDGY COCONUT BROWNIES

8 Servings

Ready in about
15 minutes

PER SERVING:
267 Calories; 15.4g Fat;
34.0g Carbs; 1.0g Protein;
27.5g Sugarss

Chop dark chocolate into small bits so it melts quickly in your microwave. For a more vibrant flavor, crumble gingersnaps over the brownies.

Ingredients

- 1/2 cup coconut oil
- 2 ounces dark chocolate
- 1 cup sugar
- 2 ½ tablespoons water
- 4 whisked eggs
- 1/4 teaspoon ground cinnamon
- 1/2 teaspoon ground anise star

- 1/4 teaspoon coconut extract
- 1/2 teaspoon vanilla extract
- 1 tablespoon honey
- 1/2 cup cake flour
- 1/2 cup desiccated coconut
- Icing sugar, to dust

Directions

1. Microwave the coconut oil along with dark chocolate. Stir in sugar, water, eggs, cinnamon, anise, coconut extract, vanilla, and honey.

2. After that, stir in the flour and coconut; mix to combine thoroughly.

3. Press the mixture into a lightly buttered baking dish. Air-bake at 355 degrees F for 15 minutes.

4. Let your brownie cool slightly; then, carefully remove from the baking dish and cut into squares. Dust with icing sugar. Bon appétit!

138. EASIEST CHOCOLATE LAVA CAKE EVER

4 Servings

Ready in about
20 minutes

PER SERVING:
549 Calories; 37.7g Fat;
47.5g Carbs; 7.1g Protein;
38.2g Sugars

With a warm, gooey center, this is a perfect gourmet dessert for any festive occasion. Only one tablespoon of honey will add a deeper flavor to your dessert.

Ingredients

- 1 cup dark cocoa candy melts
- 1 stick butter
- 2 eggs
- 4 tablespoons superfine sugar
- 1 tablespoon honey

- 4 tablespoons self-rising flour
- A pinch of kosher salt
- A pinch of ground cloves
- 1/4 teaspoon grated nutmeg
- 1/4 teaspoon cinnamon powder

Directions

1. Firstly, spray four custard cups with non-stick cooking oil.

2. Put the cocoa candy melts and butter into a small microwave-safe bowl; microwave on high for 30 seconds to 1 minute.

3. In a mixing bowl, whisk the eggs along with sugar and honey until frothy. Add it to the chocolate mix.

4. After that, add the remaining ingredients and mix to combine well. You can whisk the mixture with an electric mixer.

5. Spoon the mixture into the prepared custard cups. Air-bake at 350 degrees F for 12 minutes. Take the cups out of the Air Fryer and let them rest for 5 to 6 minutes.

6. Lastly, flip each cup upside-down onto a dessert plate and serve with some fruits and chocolate syrup. Bon appétit!

139. CHOCOLATE BANANA CAKE

10 Servings

Ready in about
30 minutes

PER SERVING:
263 Calories; 10.6g Fat;
41.0g Carbs; 4.3g Protein;
16.6g Sugars

This is one of those desserts that taste better the following day. You can omit the frosting; the cake will be great anyway.

Ingredients

- 1 stick softened butter
- 1/2 cup caster sugar
- 1 egg
- 2 bananas, mashed
- 3 tablespoons maple syrup
- 2 cups self-rising flour
- 1/4 teaspoon anise star, ground

- 1/4 teaspoon ground mace
- 1/4 teaspoon ground cinnamon
- 1/4 teaspoon crystallized ginger
- 1/2 teaspoon vanilla paste
- A pinch of kosher salt
- 1/2 cup cocoa powder

Directions

1. Firstly, beat the softened butter and sugar until well combined.

2. Then, whisk the egg, mashed banana and maple syrup. Now, add this mixture to the butter mixture; mix until pale and creamy.

3. Add in the flour, anise star, mace, cinnamon, crystallized ginger, vanilla paste, and the salt; now, add the cocoa powder and mix to combine.

4. Then, treat two cake pans with a non-stick cooking spray. Press the batter into the cake pans.

5. Air-bake at 330 degrees F for 30 minutes. To serve, frost with chocolate butter glaze.

140. BUTTER SUGAR FRITTERS

16 Servings

Ready in about
30 minutes

PER SERVING:
231 Calories; 8.2g Fat;
36.6g Carbs; 3.3g Protein;
12.8g Sugars

Fritters cook happily in an Air Fryer with the hot air making them extra crispy. If you are on your "cheat day", this recipe would be perfect for you!

Ingredients

For the dough:

- 4 cups fine cake flour
- 1 teaspoon kosher salt
- 1 teaspoon brown sugar
- 3 tablespoons butter, at room temperature
- 1 packet instant yeast
- 1 ¼ cups lukewarm water

For the Cakes:

- 1 cup caster sugar
- A pinch of cardamom
- 1 teaspoon cinnamon powder
- 1 stick butter, melted

Directions

1. Mix all the dry ingredients in a large-sized bowl; add the butter and yeast and mix to combine well.

2. Pour lukewarm water and stir to form soft and elastic dough.

3. Lay the dough on a lightly floured surface, loosely cover with greased foil and chill for 5 to 10 minutes.

4. Take the dough out of the refrigerator and shape it into two logs; cut them into 20 slices.

5. In a shallow bowl, mix caster sugar with cardamom and cinnamon.

6. Now, brush with melted butter and coat the entire slice with sugar mix; repeat with the remaining ingredients.

7. Treat the Air Fryer basket with a non-stick cooking spray. Air-fry at 360 degrees F for about 10 minutes, flipping once during the baking time. To serve, dust with icing sugar and enjoy!

141. FATHER'S DAY FRIED PINEAPPLE RINGS

6 Servings

Ready in about
10 minutes

PER SERVING:
180 Calories; 1.8g Fat;
39.4g Carbs; 2.5g Protein;
14.9g Sugars

Coconut adds rich and sophisticated flavor to this amazing dessert. Also known as beignets, these pineapple rings are crispy and tender at the same time. For a more luscious taste, soak pineapple rings in rum before dipping them in the batter.

Ingredients

- 2/3 cup all-purpose flour
- 1/3 cup rice flour
- 1/2 teaspoon baking powder
- 1/2 teaspoon baking soda
- A pinch of kosher salt
- 1/2 cup water
- 1 cup rice milk

- 1/2 teaspoon ground cinnamon
- 1/4 teaspoon ground anise star
- 1/2 teaspoon vanilla essence
- 4 tablespoons caster sugar
- 1/4 cup unsweetened flaked coconut
- 1 medium-sized pineapple, peeled and sliced

Directions

1. Mix all of the above ingredients, except the pineapple. Then, coat the pineapple slices with the batter mix, covering well.

2. Air-fry them at 380 degrees F for 6 to 8 minutes. Drizzle with maple syrup, garnish with a dollop of vanilla ice cream, and serve.

142. OATY PLUM AND APPLE CRUMBLE

6 Servings

Ready in about
20 minutes

PER SERVING:
190 Calories; 7.9g Fat;
28.7g Carbs; 1.6g Protein;
16.7g Sugars

The fruit crumble with a crunchy, oaty topping is a delectable dessert for any occasion. You can make it in bulk because it freezes well, whole or in portions.

Ingredients

- 1/4 pound plums, pitted and chopped
- 1/4 pound Braeburn apples, cored and chopped
- 1 tablespoon fresh lemon juice
- 2 ½ ounces golden caster sugar
- 1 tablespoon honey
- 1/2 teaspoon ground mace

- 1/2 teaspoon vanilla paste
- 1 cup fresh cranberries
- 1/3 cup oats
- 2/3 cup flour
- 1/2 stick butter, chilled
- 1 tablespoon cold water

Directions

1. Thoroughly combine the plums and apples with lemon juice, sugar, honey, and ground mace.

2. Spread the fruit mixture onto the bottom of a cake pan that is previously greased with non-stick cooking oil.

3. In a mixing dish, combine the other ingredients until everything is well incorporated. Spread this mixture evenly over the fruit mixture.

4. Air-bake at 390 degrees F for 20 minutes or until done.

143. BUTTER LEMON POUND CAKE

8 Servings

Ready in about
2 hours 20 minutes

PER SERVING:
227 Calories; 9.2g Fat;
34.3g Carbs; 4.2g Protein;
16.6g Sugars

Lemon is always in season, so you can enjoy this cake all year long. Adding a thick lemon glaze improves the flavor and texture of this pound cake.

Ingredients

- 1 stick softened butter
- 1/3 cup muscovado sugar
- 1 medium-sized egg
- 1 ¼ cups cake flour
- 1 teaspoon butter flavoring
- 1 teaspoon vanilla essence
- A pinch of salt
- 3/4 cup milk
- Grated zest of 1 medium-sized lemon

For the Glaze:

- 1 cup powdered sugar
- 2 tablespoons fresh squeezed lemon juice

Directions

1. In a mixing bowl, cream the butter and sugar. Now, fold in the egg and beat again.

2. Add the flour, butter flavoring, vanilla essence, and salt; mix to combine well. Afterward, add the milk and lemon zest and mix on low until everything's incorporated.

3. Evenly spread a thin layer of melted butter all around the cake pan using a pastry brush. Now, press the batter into the cake pan.

4. Bake at 350 degrees F for 15 minutes. After that, take the cake out of the Air Fryer and carefully run a small knife around the edges; invert the cake onto a serving platter. Allow it to cool completely.

5. To make the glaze, mix powdered sugar with lemon juice. Drizzle over the top of your cake and allow hardening for about 2 hours.

144. FESTIVE DOUBLE-CHOCOLATE CAKE

8 Servings

Ready in about
45 minutes

PER SERVING:
227 Calories; 12.7g Fat;
39.5g Carbs; 3.6g Protein;
24.3g Sugars

You can't go wrong with a classic chocolate cake for a holiday party! For a flavor-enriched version, don't skip the frosting.

Ingredients

- 1/2 cup caster sugar
- 1 ¼ cups cake flour
- 1 teaspoon baking powder
- 1/3 cup cocoa powder
- 1/4 teaspoon ground cloves
- 1/8 teaspoon freshly grated nutmeg
- A pinch of table salt

- 1 egg
- 1/4 cup soda
- 1/4 cup milk
- 1/2 stick butter, melted
- 2 ounces bittersweet chocolate, melted
- 1/2 cup hot water

Directions

1. Take two mixing bowls. Thoroughly combine the dry ingredients in the first bowl. In the second bowl, mix the egg, soda, milk, butter, and chocolate.

2. Add the wet mix to the dry mix; pour in the water and mix well. Butter a cake pan that fits into your Air Fryer. Pour the mixture into the baking pan.

3. Loosely cover with foil; bake at 320 degrees F for 35 minutes. Now, remove foil and bake for further 10 minutes. Frost the cake with buttercream if desired. Bon appétit!

145. APPLE AND PEAR CRISP WITH WALNUTS

6 Servings

Ready in about
25 minutes

PER SERVING:
190 Calories; 5.3g Fat;
33.1g Carbs; 3.6g Protein;
13.7g Sugars

Muscovado sugar is the surprising but superstar addition to this fruit crisp. It is a kind of brown sugar with a specific molasses flavor.

Ingredients

- 1/2 pound apples, cored and chopped
- 1/2 pound pears, cored and chopped
- 1 cup all-purpose flour
- 1/3 cup muscovado sugar
- 1/3 cup brown sugar
- 1 tablespoon butter

- 1 teaspoon ground cinnamon
- 1/4 teaspoon ground cloves
- 1 teaspoon vanilla extract
- 1/4 cup chopped walnuts
- Whipped cream, to serve

Directions

1. Arrange the apples and pears on the bottom of a lightly greased baking dish.

2. Mix the remaining ingredients, without the walnuts and the whipped cream, until the mixture resembles the coarse crumbs.

3. Spread the topping onto the fruits. Scatter chopped walnuts over all.

4. Air-bake at 340 degrees F for 20 minutes or until the topping is golden brown. Check for doneness using a toothpick and serve at room temperature topped with whipped cream.

146. FAMILY COCONUT BANANA TREAT

6 Servings

Ready in about
20 minutes

PER SERVING:
271 Calories; 6.6g Fat;
51.3g Carbs; 4.8g Protein;
19.3g Sugars

There's nothing more uplifting than an aroma of fried banana with cinnamon and coconut! This is a child-friendly recipe that your family will love.

Ingredients

- 2 tablespoons coconut oil
- 3/4 cup breadcrumbs
- 2 tablespoons coconut sugar
- 1/2 teaspoon cinnamon powder

- 1/4 teaspoon ground cloves
- 6 ripe bananas, peeled and halved
- 1/3 cup rice flour
- 1 large-sized well-beaten egg

Directions

1. Preheat a non-stick skillet over a moderate heat; stir the coconut oil and the breadcrumbs for about 4 minutes. Remove from the heat, add coconut sugar, cinnamon, and cloves; set it aside.

2. Coat the banana halves with the rice flour, covering on all sides. Then, dip them in beaten egg. Finally, roll them over the crumb mix.

3. Cook in a single layer in the Air Fryer basket at 290 degrees F for 10 minutes. Work in batches as needed.

4. Serve warm or at room temperature sprinkled with flaked coconut if desired. Bon appétit!

8 Servings | Ready in about 25 minutes | **PER SERVING:** 278 Calories; 13.1g Fat; 38.7g Carbs; 3.6g Protein; 25.6g Sugars

An old-fashioned cake makes a wonderful ending to any meal. The type of flour you use determines the texture of this dessert – a country-style with all-purpose flour, a chewy cake with self-rising flour, and light and fluffy batter with cake flour!

Ingredients

- 1 cup flour
- 1 teaspoon baking powder
- 1 cup white sugar
- 1/8 teaspoon kosher salt
- 1/4 teaspoon ground cinnamon
- 1/4 teaspoon grated nutmeg

- 1 teaspoon orange zest
- 1 stick butter, melted
- 2 eggs
- 1 teaspoon pure vanilla extract
- 1/4 cup milk
- 2 tablespoons unsweetened cocoa powder

Directions

1. Lightly grease a round pan that fits into your Air Fryer.

2. Combine the flour, baking powder, sugar, salt, cinnamon, nutmeg, and orange zest using an electric mixer. Then, fold in the butter, eggs, vanilla, and milk.

3. Add 1/4 cup of the batter to the baking pan; leave the remaining batter and stir the cocoa into it. Drop by spoonful over the top of white batter. Then, swirl the cocoa batter into the white batter with a knife.

4. Bake at 360 degrees F approximately 15 minutes. Let it cool for about 10 minutes.

5. Finally, turn the cake out onto a wire rack.

148. VANILLA AND BANANA PASTRY PUFFS

8 Servings

Ready in about
15 minutes

PER SERVING:
308 Calories; 17.1g Fat;
34.6g Carbs; 5.2g Protein;
18.4g Sugars

In this gorgeous recipe, a good replacement for banana would be fresh strawberries and even blackberries. Dust with confectioner's sugar and enjoy!

Ingredients

- 1 package (8-ounce) crescent dinner rolls, refrigerated
- 1 cup of milk
- 4 ounces instant vanilla pudding

- 4 ounces cream cheese, softened
- 2 bananas, peeled and sliced
- 1 egg, lightly beaten

Directions

1. Unroll crescent dinner rolls; cut into 8 squares.

2. Combine the milk and the pudding; whisk in the cream cheese. Divide the pudding mixture among the pastry squares. Top with the slices of banana.

3. Now, fold the dough over the filling, pressing the edges to help them seal well. Brush each pastry puff with the whisked egg.

4. Air-bake at 355 degrees F for 10 minutes. Bon appétit!

149. PARTY HAZELNUT BROWNIE CUPS

12 Servings

Ready in about
30 minutes

PER SERVING:
246 Calories; 14.5g Fat;
27.5g Carbs; 2.4g Protein;
18.6g Sugars

Take your cocktail parties to a whole new level! This recipe is a proof that brownies come from the chocolate heaven.

Ingredients

- 6 ounces semisweet chocolate chips
- 1 stick butter, at room temperature
- 1/2 cup caster sugar
- 1/4 cup brown sugar
- 2 large-sized eggs
- 1/4 cup red wine

- 1/4 teaspoon hazelnut extract
- 1 teaspoon pure vanilla extract
- 3/4 cup all-purpose flour
- 2 tablespoons cocoa powder
- 1/2 cup ground hazelnuts
- A pinch of kosher salt

Directions

1. Microwave the chocolate chips with butter.

2. Then, whisk the sugars, eggs, red wine, hazelnut and vanilla extract. Add to the chocolate mix.

3. Stir in the flour, cocoa powder, ground hazelnuts, and a pinch of kosher salt. Mix until the batter is creamy and smooth. Divide the batter among muffin cups that are coated with cupcake liners.

4. Air-bake at 360 degrees F for 28 to 30 minutes. Bake in batches and serve topped with ganache if desired.

150. SULTANA CUPCAKES WITH BUTTERCREAM ICING

6 Servings

Ready in about
25 minutes

PER SERVING:
366 Calories; 19.1g Fat;
47.4g Carbs; 2.8g Protein;
38.3g Sugars

Sultanas, also known as golden raisins, are made from seedless white-fleshed grapes and they are similar to raisins and Zante currants. There are zillion cute ideas for cupcakes; for instance, you can make a flat rosette ideal for holidays.

Ingredients

For the Cupcakes:

- 1/2 cup all-purpose flour
- 1/2 teaspoon baking soda
- 1 baking powder
- 1/8 teaspoon salt
- 1/4 teaspoon ground anise star
- 1/4 teaspoon grated nutmeg
- 1 teaspoon cinnamon
- 3 tablespoons caster sugar
- 1/2 teaspoon pure vanilla extract
- 1 egg

- 1/4 cup plain milk
- 1/2 stick melted butter
- 1/2 cup Sultanas

For the Buttercream Icing:

- 1/3 cup butter, softened
- 1 ½ cups powdered sugar
- 1 teaspoon vanilla extract
- 1/8 teaspoon salt
- 2 tablespoons milk
- A few drop food coloring

Directions

1. Take two mixing bowls. Thoroughly combine the dry ingredients for the cupcakes into the first bowl. In another bowl, whisk the vanilla extract, egg, milk, and melted butter.

2. To form a batter, add the wet milk mixture to the dry flour mixture. Fold in Sultanas and gently stir to combine. Ladle the batter into the prepared muffin pans.

3. Air-bake at 390 degrees F for 15 minutes.

4. Meanwhile, to make the Buttercream Icing, beat the butter until creamy and fluffy. Gradually add the sugar and beat well.

5. Then, add the vanilla, salt, and milk, and mix until creamy. Afterward, gently stir in food coloring. Frost your cupcakes and enjoy!

AIR FRYER COOKING TABLE

		Min-max amount (oz.)	Time (min.)	Temp. °F	Shake halfway	Extra information
Thin frozen fries		11-43oz	9-19	360	✓	
Thick frozen fries		11-43oz	12-22	360	✓	
Homemade fries		11oz 32oz 21oz 43oz	15 22 18 25	360	✓	Soak 30 min./dry/Tbsp oil 1/4 tbsp-11oz 3/4 tbsp-32oz 1/2 tbsp-21oz 1 tbsp-43oz
Potato wedges		11oz 21oz 32oz	18-21 24	360	✓	Soak 30 min./dry/Tbsp oil 1/4 tbsp-11oz 1/2 tbsp-21oz 3/4 tbsp-32oz
Potato cubes		11oz 21oz 32oz	12-18	360	✓	Soak 30 min./dry/Tbsp oil 1/4 tbsp-11oz 1/2 tbsp-21oz 3/4 tbsp-32oz
Cheese sticks		4-16oz	8-10	360	✓	Use oven ready
Chicken nuggets		14oz	6	330/390	✓	Use oven ready
Fish sticks		4oz/12oz	8/10	390		Use oven ready
Steak		4oz/21oz	5min 360+4min 150 6min 360 +4min 150	360		
Pork chops		4oz/14oz	6/7	360		
Hamburger		4oz/14oz	6/7	360		
Chicken wings		3oz/21oz	18-22	360		
Drumsticks		3oz/21oz	10min 390+10min 320	390		
Chicken breast		4-oz/28oz	8min 290+6min 360 8min 290 +8min 360	360		
Cake		24oz	30	320		

Lisa Olson is an Austin-based food blogger and recipe developer who has attended the Auguste Escoffier School of Culinary Arts in Austin, Texas. She has now written several cookbooks, some of which are already up for sale on Amazon and more are on their way.

When she is not cooking in the kitchen you can usually find her wandering at the Barton Creek Farmers' Market or spending time at home with her two lovely little daughters, who also help her in the kitchen sometimes. Lisa Olson lives in Austin, Texas with her family and their dachshund Rocky.

With her books she wants to help you cook healthy and delicious meals for your family and make the process fun and easy, so you can really enjoy it.

You can visit her website: lisaolsoncooking.com

Lightning Source UK Ltd.
Milton Keynes UK
UKHW050005150922
408875UK00003B/45

9 780998 770307